# BOOTS
# OF
# WAR

# BOOTS OF WAR

Unforgettable experiences from a front line
surgeon during Operation Iraqi Freedom

## JAY T. BISHOFF MD

ISBN: 1461116813
ISBN-13: 9781461116813
Library of Congress Control Number: 2010914632

*This book is dedicated to*
*all those who wear*
*or have worn*
*the boots of war.*

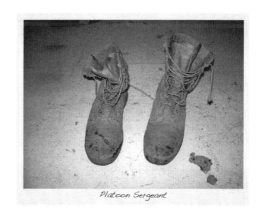

Platoon Sergeant

# ACKNOWLEDGEMENT

I want to acknowledge the assistance of
Mr. Groomer (Bill), my high school English teacher.
Even though many years have passed since graduation,
his teaching continues to have a great influence on me.
His tireless efforts in manuscript revision
and photo editing made this project a reality.

# TABLE OF CONTENTS

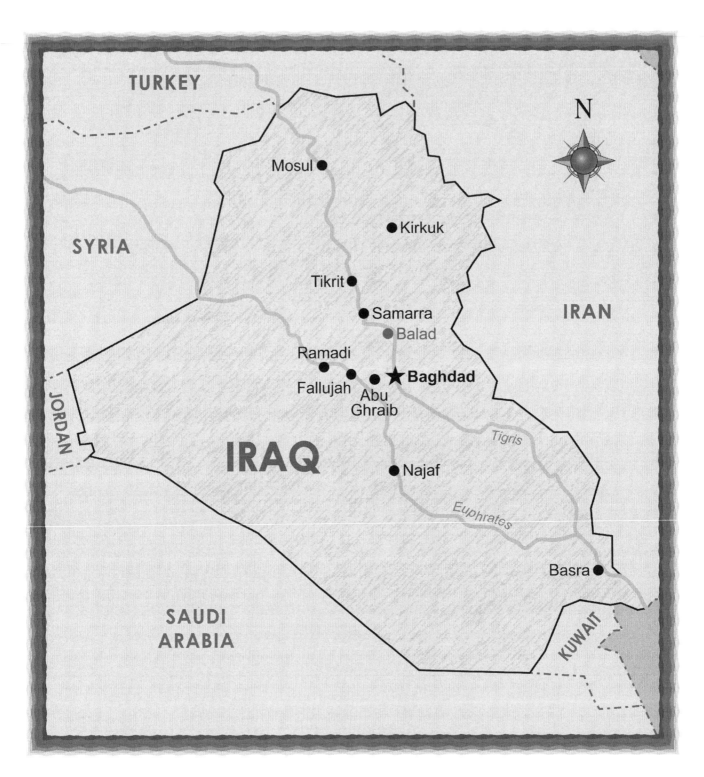

# PREFACE

In January 2006, two weeks before the start of my tour in Iraq, I was at a local bookstore with my children.  I was thumbing through a magazine depicting the major world events of the year 2005 in review. As I perused the graphic pictures of hurricane, tornado and tsunami devastation, my attention was drawn to a simple photo of a folded American flag and a fallen soldier's boots, sitting empty on a wooden platform. No title was given, and no explanation needed. The visual impact of that simple photo had an immediate and deep emotional impact on me. As I stood staring at the photo, noting the details of the hastily built battlefield memorial, I was reminded that I was on my way to war and that the fallen soldier's boots could be my boots or the boots of anyone sent in support of Operation Iraqi Freedom.

After I arrived in Iraq I frequently thought of those empty boots and the soldier who had made the ultimate sacrifice to serve his country. Soon I began to notice many different boots worn by those around me. They came to represent the different wartime services and sacrifices everyone was making to further world peace. There were the soiled combat boots of the front line soldier (risking his life daily) which he referred to as his "lucky boots," the vascular surgeon's black wing tip dress shoes worn only in the operating room, the nurses' clogs, the boots of a soldier desperate in his search of the base for the group of visiting NFL cheerleaders, and the bare feet of a wounded Iraqi civilian – all telling a unique story. I felt the stories needed to be recorded and shared so I took pictures. The end result was the poster, a photo essay, entitled *Boots of War.* Most of the pictures are now part of this book and a written explanation of the photo essay, along with the poster are included in one of the chapters.

The written accounts of the war come from my daily journal entries detailing my own personal experiences, which at times were repetitive and mundane and at other times exhilarating and exhausting. For me these personal experiences are more than simply stories.

While in Iraq I had the great privilege of caring, not only for the medical, but for the spiritual welfare of some of America's finest men and women. In addition to my responsibilities as a urological surgeon assigned to the 332nd Expeditionary Medical Group (EMDG) hospital, I was called to be a "Group Leader" for the Church of Jesus Christ of Latter-day Saints, or Mormons.  Several spiritual experiences are recounted, because they were born of that calling and my deep religious convictions.

In addition to providing medical care to the American and coalition forces, it was my privilege and pleasure to care for many Iraqi civilians and Iraqi officials. In the hospital I had the chance to develop personal relationships with many of my patients, especially the seriously wounded soldiers, many of whom stayed at our hospital for a week before they were ready to return to their previous stations or duties. As they shared their stories with me, I learned a deeper meaning of duty and responsibility. They broadened my understanding of words and concepts that I thought I already understood. After all, I am a surgeon, and surgeons know sacrifice, responsibility, and duty. But these young men and women taught me that I did not fully understand the depth and power of those words.

After addressing the pressing urological issues that brought patients (often at great risk) to see me, I asked them this simple question, "What is the wildest thing that has happened to you here in Iraq?" Then I sat back and listened to stories too wild to make up. Almost daily, there were inspiring experiences that members of the Armed Forces shared with me. I was impressed by the freshness and honesty with which they related the significant events of their lives, so at night I would relax by writing and reflecting on those experiences and now I share them with you.

# INTRODUCTION

At the start of the U.S. military involvement in the first Gulf War (1991), I was a fourth year medical student on rotation in France. French Surgeon General Daniel Rignault had arranged a general surgery rotation for me with Professor Jean Louis Paille at the Hopital D'Instruction des Armees Val de Grace in Paris. It was here that Professor Paille taught me the value of the individual and the physician's sacred obligation to the patient regardless of race or religion.

As Iraq invaded Kuwait, the French government deported the entire staff of the Iraqi embassy, including the ambassador and his family, with the exception of one person. The ambassador's wife was in the Val de Grace Hospital, as Dr. Paille had just removed part of her cancerous colon. I was on rounds with a large group of physicians, nurses, physical therapists, nutritionists and social workers. One of the physicians in training was presenting a patient to the entire group, elaborating on the post-operative day two details, such as colectomy, no flatus, tolerating sips of liquids, etc. In a nearby hallway a ruckus of yelling and screaming arose.

Several nurses rushed to fetch Dr. Paille. We all followed him to the room of the Iraqi ambassador's wife, where a large group of the French police had assembled, apparently with the goal of physically removing her from the hospital. Dr. Paille quickly forced his way through the crowd outside her door pushing uniformed police and French officials in suits out of his way. He closed the patient's door, and standing fearlessly in front of the crowd, his long white coat flowing nearly to the ground, arms on his chest, yelled at the police.

"You will not take this patient out of my hospital until I say you can. She leaves when she is ready for discharge. *And, she is not ready!* She leaves when I say she leaves. If you take her today, you take her over my dead body!"

As if hard-wired thoughts had programmed their movements, the civilain officials in suits and the uniformed police reached for their weapons simultaneously. The crowd spontaneously moved back a step. I was standing in the very back of this large group, but being taller than most I could see that they were actually going to shoot Dr. Paille in order to get the last Iraqi official out of the country. Fortunately, one of the officials in a suit lifted his hand as if to signal a halt to the pending massacre of one of France's finest physicians and surgeons. The armed police holstered their weapons, and we all breathed a great sigh of relief.

The official who had raised his hand and stopped the altercation simply said, "We will be back" and turned to leave.

Before the group could disband, Dr. Paille looked over the entire crowd, but focused directly on me. As he started to speak the crowd froze. Looking and pointing at me he said, "Dr. Bishoff, patient care trumps politics every time. . . . Every time."

The last of the police and suited officials turned and left the building.

We returned to rounds almost as if nothing happened, but in fact something had happened, and I knew I would never really be the same person or surgeon again. I wondered if any of the witnesses to this brief event could ever again be the same. We would forever have more courage. Several days later the Iraqi ambassador's wife was ready for discharge and was immediately deported from France.

Figure I. At the completion of his general surgery rotation in Paris, France fourth year medical student Jay T. Bishoff, receives a silver tray from Professor Jean Louis Paille at the Hopital D'Instruction des Armees Val de Grace in Paris.

Two weeks later Dr. Paille asked me to help him with a large box that had arrived at his office. We pulled from it the most stunning Persian carpet I had ever seen. It was sixteen by twenty feet. We spread it on the floor in the hallway and admired its craftsmanship, exquisite detail and cashmere softness. The carpet was essentially perfect and so impressed Dr. Paille, that he announced it would be framed and hung on his wall at home —a gift to Dr. Paille and all of France from the Iraqi ambassador and his grateful wife.

Little did I know that many years later Dr. Paille's words would echo in my mind as I cared for Iraqis—civilians, military, insurgents, terrorists, and those who would have done us harm given the chance.

*"Patient care trumps politics every time. . . . Every time."*

For Every Foot

# Chapter I

———

# HARD TASKED

Training is the backbone of the military. In fact, just yesterday here in Iraq one of our commanders said, "We can never be too busy to train!" Since we are actually in Iraq and very busy doing what we've been trained to do, all I could think was, "Wow, never too busy to train? Never mind that actual gunshot wounds were arriving every few hours, interspersed with burns, Humvee rollovers, kidney stones, miscellaneous traumatic injuries, IED bomb explosions, uncontrolled nose bleeds, heart attacks, poisoning, and much more are pretty good training for everyone!" Nevertheless, the commander was as good as her word; we were "never too busy to train."

In many ways a training exercise for a commander is like a surgical procedure for a surgeon; the pre-operative work-up, the planning, is intellectually stimulating. The surgical procedure, or exercise, is not only interesting and fun to do, it is educational. The post-operative care and follow-up, as in the case of training debriefing, highlights the final results and leads to discoveries that help us improve our performance.

Preparing for deployment to war requires training, but most surgeons don't see the same value in wartime training that a military commander sees. A surgeon's idea of training is to perform actual surgeries under realistic situations. Non-surgical training is dull, silly, and even unnecessary to the surgeon who is busy training to perform battlefield surgical procedures. The other types of training seem, for the most part, to be less immediately applicable. Despite efforts to avoid non-surgical training everyone in the military ends up knee-deep in it because everyone, at least everyone in the Air Force, is supposed to be on "mobility."

Technically, being on mobility means being ready to leave with only twenty-four hours notice to anywhere in the world. So when one is on mobility, a bag or two filled with personal items— toothbrush, comb, socks, underwear, batteries, yards of parachute cord, duct tape—is always ready.

Since finishing my residency and post-doctorate fellowship in 1998, I have been on mobility and yes, I've always had a personal bag ready, sitting in the closet upstairs in my office, smelling of the Dial soap secured deep inside it. When the call came, I didn't know when I might get more soap, toothpaste, socks or duct tape.

Occasionally, those of us on mobility are called in at a moment's notice for a "bag drag"—an inspection of one's personal bag. A check list is carefully used to mark off the items and ensure compliance. In the middle of a busy clinic or surgery schedule, the bag drag does not bring much joy to the surgeon who is busy training for surgery. There are stories from the Vietnam War about soldiers and airmen being called in for a bag drag in the middle of the night, being loaded on an airplane and flown around the area before returning to base. Now and then the bag dragger would actually put his bag on a plane and fly to Vietnam. Now that is a real exercise! So with that possibility, I always kept my bag ready.

Military commanders themselves are very well trained in making up lists of things to train for: biological or chemical attack, use of chemical protective suits, gas masks, weapons training (even surgeons are required to train with the M-16 and M-9), counter terrorism, computer security, weapon handling, first-aid, self-aid, buddy care, rules of engagement, human rights training, human trafficking, the law of armed conflict, and review of the Geneva Convention, just to mention a few that readily come to mind. Wartime training for the surgeon goes on all year long at a steady unending pace, not to mention practicing medical procedures and operations.

When the call to deploy arrives, the surgeon graduates from being on mobility to the category of being hard tasked, which is really mobility on steroids. Suddenly there is the red Hard Tasked, stamp boldly emblazoned on your paperwork. New checklists are handed out. While the old checklist of things to do and keep current was one or two pages, the new one is like the organic chemistry handout you received in college. You wonder how anyone could possibly ever be ready to leave to help fight the war, this or any war. Did Eisenhower and Patton have a checklist? Did they wait in long lines? Suddenly, I really wanted to be in a Special Forces unit, I bet they don't have ten page checklists. I am certain that, like me, they have their personal bags ready, and they go when called. Even if I were to cancel my entire clinic and surgery schedule for two weeks, I still wouldn't have time to complete the list. This is something that those merely on mobility won't understand until their turn actually comes.

When you are hard tasked, all of your training needs to be current. All training programs have expiration dates, and if you let any expire you are recycled back to make it current. It is no fun repeating something you have already crossed off your list.

"Are you sure my training has expired? It seems like just yesterday that I was in the gas chamber," can be heard in different variations coming from everywhere.

Because you are hard tasked, you need a recent physical exam, a copy of your medical records, a health-risk assessment (probably done by an overweight staff sergeant instructing you to exercise three times a week, and warning you about the adverse effects of tobacco on the human body. Unfortunately, you can't concentrate on his message because of the strong stench of cigarette smoke on his breath.)

"Done! I understand! I will!! Now, please sign item number fifty on my checklist so I can move on to the next task."

The next stop is an office that is probably closed or manned by people either at lunch, mobility training, or standing in another line because they are also hard tasked. Progress on your checklist is monitored by having it checked and your progress recorded. Finishing the checklist takes long enough that once you think you are done with it, the checklist checkers inform you that an item or two or three have expired, so back you go to the list, but this time with renewed determination not to let the list get the best of you.

Ouch! Don't forget a current dental exam, films, teeth cleaning, and the shots. You have to love the shots! You thought your immunizations were up to date, but the new checklist has surprises—anthrax in the right arm (three shots, but the good news is that you will finally be immune to exposure when you get home and get the final shot). You also get a smallpox shot in the left arm, which includes regular dressing changes while a big pustule forms, drains for a week, and finally scabs over. And by all means don't let the smallpox dressings touch anything in your household, bathtub, pool, or hot tub, or everyone dies of smallpox.

Next, typhoid and yellow fever have expired, and you missed your flu shot. Go back to immunizations. They can give you those today unless the retirees have used up all the flu shots or there is a run on yellow fever vaccinations, which means check back next week.

Your own Last Will and Testament needs to be updated, insurance checked, security clearance reviewed, renewed or started, finance briefing, family support center briefing (only three pages left and the checklist seems complete). But wait, what did the list checker just say? "Good job sir, now you are ready, but your checklist will have to be checked across base by the final list checkers." Wow, there is a list checker who checks the list after it has been cleared by the list checker, and she only checks lists by appointment, which she sets and emails to you. The only problem is that the date is the same day I am scheduled to do a kidney transplant for a family that has been waiting two months to have the surgery. Thank God the checklist checker has a family member on dialysis waiting for a kidney. She is suddenly sympathetic enough to grant a rare change in the final checklist checking. Did General Washington have a check list?

Being hard tasked is not all bad. It also means you get free stuff. During the hard task process there is an equipment issue and lots of equipment, including:

    2x big green indestructible bags
    4 desert camouflage shirts
    4 desert camouflage pants
    One pair desert Gortex boots
    Desert 8 point cap
    Desert Boonie hat
    Unit patches CENTAF

Name tapes and USAF tapes
Gortex desert jacket with polar fleece liner
Gortex desert pants with polar fleece liner
Cold weather underwear, shirt, gloves, socks (8 pair)
Desert goggles clear lens and tinted lens
DCU Helmut cover
DEET bug spray
Reflective belt
Wool blanket, one each
Black watch cap
Kevlar helmet
Individual body armor with thyroid and groin flap, one each
WileyX sunglasses with tinted and clear lenses

Some of the equipment is not really yours, but on loan to you:

Bag of chemical exposure gear
Complete MOPP (Mission Oriented Protective Posture) gear
Gas mask
Sleeping bag
Mess kit
Web gear canteen

There are a lot more necessities, but I think you get the idea.

Soon it dawns on you, "Wait, why do I need all of this free stuff?"

Eventually, the hard tasked get their orders. Nothing really happens until then, but once you have orders, it usually means you really are leaving. Now, in addition to one personal bag, three additional bags are filled and kept ready in the closet at home. The desert uniforms are readied and adorned with all the necessary patches and name tapes. Uniforms are treated with bug repellant by soaking them in DEET-filled plastic bags overnight, then hanging them out to air dry. This confers immunity to bug bites for about fifty cold-water washes.

Two weeks prior to the departure window, all hard tasked start to wear the desert camouflage uniform (DCU). Patients in the halls of the hospital who have lived through being hard tasked during World War II, Korea, Vietnam, or the first Gulf War look at you with understanding and at the same time a look that says "good luck." The hard tasked walking the halls stirs images and memories they have long suppressed and rarely discuss. Those memories occasionally surface as tears in eyes of patients as they offer words of encouragement and advice. "Bishoff, keep your ass down!"

Your dog tags clink as you walk through the halls of the hospital greeting others wearing the desert uniform. The hard tasked are finally set apart from the rest who are merely on mobility.

*Unit Travel Director*

———

# Chapter 2

# THE BUMPS IN THE ROAD ST

After months of training and checklists, 140 medics and their 560 bags that weigh just less than sixty pounds each are ready to go to war. The commander instructs everyone to show up at 0500 hours January 13, 2006. Once all four bags are packed and goodbyes said, a rumor spreads through the hospital that the plane is grounded for repairs and we will be delayed for twenty-four hours. The readiness office phone is busy and no call is delivered to confirm the rumor. Finally, in the evening the rumor is confirmed: "It is a NO GO for the 13th. NEW SHOW TIME 14 January Saturday at 1200 hrs."

Everything is ready, so for the first time in many years there is no rush and nothing much to do. Free time takes on a whole new meaning.

### Why Are We Getting More Gloves?

After a wonderful day of rest and playing, it is time to go. My wife and I prepare for a fun and animated drive to the hospital with all of the kids in the car. Everyone in my family seems to want to say something.

I feel like I should teach more of life's vital lessons, in case I don't have a chance to squeeze them in later. What if I die in the war? Have I said all that I need to say? Have I taught the kids all they need to know to get through this life? I panic.

"Okay, kids, listen up. If I can share one more piece of advice with you, it is this: Throughout your entire life you need to make sure you are (1) where you are supposed to be, (2) when you are supposed to be there, and (3) doing what you are supposed to be doing. Brandon and Tanner, for you two that means being at the sacrament table for Sunday church services early enough to get the sacrament ready, and to pass it. It is a sacred responsibility so act like you understand that fact. On Wednesday night, youth church activities, it means more than showing up so remember number three: it is not enough to just show up, and then be disagreeable about being there and not participating in the activity. It means. . . ."

"Okay, Dad, we got it. But we thought the most important lesson was (1) we have to know where you are, (2) who you are with, and (3) what you are doing all the time."

"Yes, that also."

t. We swear you said that the key to success in life was, 'That which we persist in doing easier to do, not that the nature of the task has changed, but that your ability to do the s increased.'"

"That is true as well. Okay, maybe you know all you need to know," I conceded. "Anyway, we are now at the hospital."

When we arrived, there was a long line of cars waiting, each in turn to unload everyone's packed bags. I was surprised to see how helpful all the bag handlers were. The guys on mobility would not let us touch our own bags; instead they quickly and happily unloaded the car and moved our bags to the waiting trucks.

Figure 2. 14 January 2006. Drop off at Wilford Hall Medical Center San Antonio, Texas. From left to right, back row: Tanner, Jay, Brandon, and Kris. Front row: Maddi and Lauren.

I felt a surprising sense of urgency. Could we really be leaving right away? It sure felt like it. This is going to be like the airport, I thought. They are taking care of everything.

We parked the car, took some pictures, and went to the auditorium and were told to come back in two hours. I was thrilled that Brandon and all of the kids had cleared their schedules to bring me to the hospital. There was free food, candy, popcorn, and drinks, like a big going away party! I noticed that my family was starting to show some interest in the process, so we slowed down and enjoyed the party for a while, that is until the snacks became only teasers to our roaring appetites. We hurried to the cafeteria and had lots of greasy fries, burgers, and corn dogs.

Finally, after about two hours I hugged my wife and kids once again. They gave me a family photo album that I tucked away in the last space left in my carry-on bag. I told them all how much I loved them and then turned around to walk back to the auditorium. There was a short meeting, and then we were dismissed and told to come back at eight p.m. You are now wondering exactly what we were wondering: why did we show up at twelve o'clock to come back at eight o'clock? There were no good answers, but our families were gone, so I went to my office in the urology clinic and finished what little work was left to complete.

At eight p.m. we received word that the plane was scheduled to leave at midnight. The same thing crossed each of our minds: I am certainly glad I arrived twelve hours early, so I would not get left behind.

"When we call your name, sign in, and pick up a pair of leather gloves to take in your carry-on bag," barked the first sergeant.

That's strange. We already have a pair of leather gloves in our packed bags. Why another pair of stiff leather gloves?

## To Get to Iraq, You Go to Virginia and Turn Right

At about 2000 hours, we boarded buses that took us to the readiness office across base, where we were weighed and logged in to get ready for boarding the airplane. Lunch was served, and we enjoyed the ensuing three hour wait. There were two waiting rooms. In one room a surprisingly violent and vulgar gangster R-rated movie was playing. I picked up my stuff and moved to the other room along with a large group of others frankly offended by the content. A better choice of movie, PG-13, was showing in the room we moved into.

After a short time, carry-on bags were measured and checked once again. There were no briefings, just more waiting. At 2300 hours the buses pulled up.

A long line of people from the hospital and base waited to say goodbye and; no, wait, they want to shake our hands. The people on mobility, two-hundred strong, were there to shake the hard-tasked hands. High fives would have been easier and quicker, but it was a wonderful send off. It was midnight on a cold, windy, dark Saturday, but all those people on mobility came out to see us off, including the Air Education and Training Command (AETC) General and the hospital commander along with their wives and children. We clambered aboard the busses and were finally on the road to Kelly Air Force Base.

During the flight, we were finally trusted with the actual schedule. At first the commander said we would not be getting off the plane in Virginia, where we were to pick-up additional medical personnel from other bases to make a complete hospital. It took about six hours to get to Virginia, and the commander wisely changed his mind and let people off the plane in Virginia for the three-hour delay.

Once we were back on the plane, there was a long flight to Ireland and another two-hour lay-over, with a two beer limit. After Ireland it was a long trip to Qatar Al Udeid Air Base. Forty-eight hours after the plane left San Antonio, we were finally in the gulf and close to Iraq. It was January 14, 2006, and finally our mission had begun.

Tired, grimy, and sore we packed into a tent to hear confusing briefings and to split up into smaller groups, some going to Kuwait, some to Al Udeid, the rest to Balad and Baghdad. Most of the group lists were wrong, and many people were surprised to see their names on a list sending them to the wrong country. How could transportation possibly mess this up so completely? Now there was confusion in the minds of 144 medics and about thirty non-medics, all caused by bad lists that seemed to randomly assign people to one base or another with no rhyme or reason. Then to make things worse, all of the commanders had been siphoned off from the small groups to take an early flight together. The rest of us, all 144, were going the next day, or the day after that, but no one really knew when. Once the "planners" found out that their lists were screwed-up, they realized they had a major problem on their hands. We did not have seventy people going to Balad, like transportation had planned; instead we needed space for 144, more than double the assigned amount.

Suddenly, getting to Balad did not really matter. No one was going anywhere because there were 560 bags that needed to be unloaded from a flatbed trailer and piled in a dirt and dust-filled baggage yard.

The Sergeant in charge called out, "The troop commander will be Lieutenant Colonel Bishoff. Sir, where are you? I need you to send everyone out to unload the bag trailer. In the yard, on the double!"

"All right! Grab the new gloves graciously given to you by the United States Air Force and follow me," I barked in my best military commander's voice. "We have bags to move."

Travel arrangements would have to wait, because we had to move all the bags from a large semi-trailer and sort them according various final destinations.

What happened to all of those nice bag handlers back at Lackland Air Force Base? I wondered. Since the mobility guys were no longer present, it was time for us soft-handed surgeons to don the stiff leather gloves and actually put them to use moving 560 bags weighing awfully close to sixty pounds each. We stacked the bags into huge random piles, and then the trailer pulled out to another C-17 and was filled with the next load of green bags.

Our problem was compounded when a large group deplaned to join our original group. A transport officer yelled to me, "Sir there are more of you than we anticipated, so you need to split everyone up into groups of no more than twenty. We may need to move in smaller groups to get everyone to Balad. Have everyone separate out their own bags. Check all 120 of your M-16s and all forty-six of your 9-mm weapons into the armory, then take out everything you will need for a 72 hour stay."

So out we went, tired and grimy. We were now covered with a layer of a sand and dust mixture fine enough to penetrate even tight military zippers on the bags. All the bags were moved, sorted, and moved again into nine tidy piles. Seventy-two-hour survival kits were assembled, and we finally boarded buses bound for base housing and, after fifty-three hours, some sleep.

The beds at Qatar felt wonderful, but the showers felt much better. For two days I checked the schedule and worked the transportation system to try to get us all to Balad. Eventually, we sought intervention from the base Colonel who called the Balad base commander, a one-star general. He finally put a stop to the wait. There were 150 medics in Balad waiting for us to relieve them, and we were stuck in Qatar. The prior rotation, 150 medics, had faithfully served their time through Thanksgiving, Christmas, and New Years and they were more than ready to go home.

Figure 3. Qatar Al Udeid Air Base. Forty-eight hours after the plane left San Antonio we were checking in cases of M-16s and 9 mm pistols.

Channels were eventually cleared, and we were finally manifested for a C-17 flight to Iraq. We showed up at the passenger terminal hours before the flight so that we could once again move all the bags and pack them onto pallets to be loaded onto the C-17. We were forced to wait and sleep in the outdoor tent-covered PAX terminals for three more hours. Finally, just before dark, the C-17 was loaded, engines roared to life, then abruptly, stopped. The bad news was not warmly received: "Ramp closed in Balad. We will be in holding for another hour."

Almost two hours later, the plane lifted off, and we were finally on our way to Iraq to help in the fight. The loadmaster had to shake me awake to ask me about the transportation manifest, which indicated that we were short four people. I checked my personal manifest; it was correct and theirs was not. After convincing the loadmaster that all were present and accounted for, I looked around the plane. Everyone was sound asleep.

Figure 4. C-17 aircraft loaded with the 332nd hospital staff over Baghdad just before landing.

"Balad on the right side," announced the pilot. "We will be landing shortly. Everyone must wear full body armor for the descent into Balad."

I stood to see Balad with lots of lights mainly in the center, but spotty on the outskirts.

The plane descended quickly towards the base airfield. Once on the ground we were told what to do in case of a mortar attack. Buses quickly took us from the dark runway to "in-processing." Several nurses quickly approached me. They had not eaten all day and were visibly upset about it. They not-too-subtly suggested that I put off the processing until we all ate. They were even more upset when I not-too-subtly sent them back to fill out paperwork and begin in-processing immediately.

After an hour of paperwork and in-processing, we lumbered onto buses to take us to base housing. On the way to housing, we encountered yet another problem: our bags were on a big trailer that had been unloaded in the wrong area. The mistake could not immediately be rectified because the trailer had gone back to the airfield for more bags. Worse yet, the housing units we thought we were going to were closed. Apparently they don't in-process newcomers after 1800 hours, and it was now 2400 hours. All 560 bags were in a disorganized heap on an outdoor basketball court in the wrong housing area. Where are the outgoing and new commanders? I wondered.

I called the mission control center at the hospital and told them about our problem. No one had any answers. The only thing that could have made the situation worse was rain. It was already cold and the rainy season had started. It was now sprinkling. The base commander arrived to welcome us, but it soon became apparent that he was not going to be much help. I called the outgoing "first shirt" and requested his presence. The first shirt's plan had unraveled, and there was no backup plan.

After many phone calls and orders, trucks from the hospital arrived to help with bags. Our various groups were shuttled to temporary army housing. After three hours we arrived at temporary housing, sorting and moving bags again, this time trying to find all four of our own. At last, sleep.

In the morning we awoke and moved our bags once again. Two of the surgeons had left us the night before. They were picked up by their replacements at the hospital, leaving their bags for others to move and secure. I was steamed. While we sat in the cold, they went to dinner and then to bed, leaving us to move their stuff. The next day I was thrilled to learn that after dinner, just after they had gone to bed, they were awakened and sent to the hospital to be on call and ended up operating all night.

Finally, almost a week after leaving San Antonio, we were in a strange, scary and unfamiliar area, Balad Air Base, home of the 332d Expeditionary Medical Group (EMDG) our new hospital for the next 120 days. It was a dismal sight. All vegetation except eucalyptus trees had been destroyed by trucks, tires, and bombs. Landscaped in dust and dirt, decorated in plain gray cement T-barriers, everything looked like everything else on base. There were very few original buildings of cement or brick and precious few markings.

The first day at work Colonel Steve Lynch and Staff Sergeant Matt Pring showed us around the hospital. They introduced us to the best part of the entire tent city, the urology clinic, which they had furnished with refrigerator, couch, desk, computer and cable TV.

Figure 5. The urology teams. From left to right: Col Steve Lynch, Sergeant Matthew Pring, Sergeant Bobby Sechler, Lt Col Jay Bishoff

Lynch and I started seeing patients in the clinic, several of whom needed stone treatment. Later in the afternoon, we made a small bit of medical, and surgical history by performing the first flexible ureteroscopy with laser lithotripsy and basket stone extraction of a kidney stone in a forward combat hospital. However, few would recognize the significance, since most of the focus was on trauma surgery and neurosurgery. Nevertheless, we quietly continued to treat about one-hundred and twenty kidney stone patients in four months and returned all to duty without leaving the theater of operation. Most patients were returned to duty in seven days. Prior to this advance, made during our rotation, kidney stone patients were air evacuated to Germany and often back to Walter Reed or Brooke Army Medical center if the schedule was too busy in Germany to treat them in a timely fashion. During all of the travel the soldiers were still suffering from the intense unbearable pain unique to kidney stones.

Once treated state side, it could take several months to get the soldiers back to their units in Iraq. There is little redundancy in personnel deployed to fight the war, so while absent, others had to carry the weight of the missing soldiers. The treatment of kidney stones was a nice diversion from our share of severe urethral trauma, penis and scrotal gunshot wounds, ureter injures, and bladder ruptures.

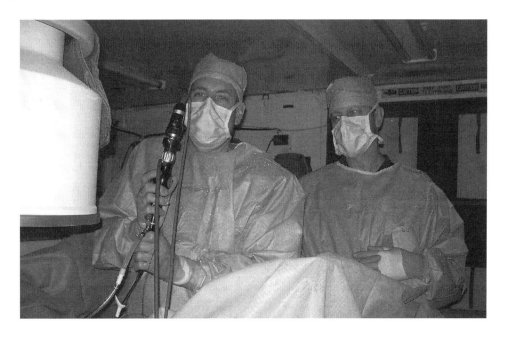

Figure 6. The first ureteroscopy, laser lithotripsy, basket stone extraction procedure ever performed in a forward combat field hospital performed by Lt Col Jay Bishoff and Col Steve Lynch.

Mental Health Nurse

# Chapter 3

———

# WHAT ARE CONDITIONS LIKE THERE

Many of my family and friends asked about my circumstances in general so, in response, I sent them this letter, early in my rotation. My brother had asked if being in Iraq was like the old television show M\*A\*S\*H, to which I bristled a bit simply because this was real, no actors, actual blood and real human soldiers suffering through some incredibly terrible wounds. As I grew into my new role and began to see and seek humor and relief from the daily stress of reality, I would come to realize that it was in fact very much like M\*A\*S\*H.

*Dear Family,*

*Sorry it has taken a while to get back to you. After sitting in the auditorium for 12 hours on 14 January we finally left at midnight 15 January 2006. First we flew to Norfolk Virginia, Ireland and finally Al Udeid Qatar, where we stayed in for two days before they could move us out to Balad Iraq. Our hospital is in tents, but surrounded by 18 ft cement walls. I have included several photos. We are located in an old Iraqi air base that is about 5 x 2 miles. The entire base is surrounded by guard towers and cement walls. It is difficult to tell where you are because everything looks the same—gray concrete. The hospital is a busy place with injuries and problems of all types. Improvised explosive devices and gunshot wounds are common, but so are the usual problems of this type of environment, like falls, back sprains, crushed fingers/toes, lots of kidney stones and even an occasional unintentional discharge of a weapon resulting in a hole in the foot. Last week someone accidentally dropped a shock grenade in the back of a Humvee. His battle buddies were not amused.*

*Weather: 1) Two types cold and rainy with temperatures around 35°F and rain with lots and lots of mud. It was a blast for my dual suspension mountain bike with full mud fenders large puddles small lakes all around the place and more mud than even 12 year old Deacons could enjoy. 2) Dust storms that come on like cotton candy and cover everything inside and outside the hospital. Gary (my brother the hospital pharmacist) the hospital environment (Inside the hospital) would instantly stoke an entire JACHO*

*(Joint Commission on Accreditation of Healthcare Organizations) inspection team. They sweep the dust in the halls after a dust storm which results in essentially two dust storms for the price of one.*

*In mass casualty situations, we have two patients in each operating room for a total of 6 patients in the OR at one time (only 3 ORs). The pharmacy is always on edge because narcotics fly off the shelves and can be found in every medics pocket, pants, and shirts. It is essentially impossible to keep track of them in the usual fashion.*

*Food: More food than you can imagine. All free and as much as a fat man can stuff inside, including Baskin Robins ice cream. I am amazed that anyone can lose weight here, but somehow they do. The dining facility is full of weapons on the floor and lots of body armor. On a daily basis the infantry coming to us for care reminds us how lucky we are. They get 3-4 hot meals a week and eat MRE's for the rest. The majority of our Marines and soldiers are living in tents, but many units live in buildings deserted by the Iraqis after our invasion.*

*Accommodations: Well it is true rank has advantages. Lt Col (that's me) and above get their own room and share a bathroom with shower and toilet with an adjoining room. If you are Major or below you have a roommate and you get to walk to the bathroom and shower as well.*

*Entertainment: Movies at the theater, occasional USO celebrity, NFL cheerleaders, and Jesse James from Monster Garage was a big hit. He stayed for 2 weeks and worked in the shop that repairs and rebuilds trucks and Humvee after they get blasted with improvised explosive devices. The country duo Montgomery Gentry were here recently.*

*Exercise: Lots of weight rooms and aerobic exercise on treadmills, etc. All open 24 hours a day.*

*Church: The Church of Jesus Christ of Latter-day Saints Stake President from the Arabian Peninsula called me to be the group leader for one of the three Mormon Church groups that meets here on base. The first Sunday we had 16 present, but they expect the ward to grow to 60 people over the next 4 months. Family home evening on Monday nights is a service project where we visit the soldiers on the ward and on Wednesday, there is an activity night. Everyone comes in, puts their M-16s and 9MM on the ground while we play games or watch movies.*

*Well the choppers are landing so I will close for now. In the short time I have been here I have found it very rewarding caring for the troops who as we say are at the tip of the spear in this conflict. They are among the bravest young men and women you will ever find. They did not choose to come here, but because it is their job they are here. They work "outside the wire" of protection on the base where medics are not allowed to go. They patrol the streets of Iraq. They seek out and engage insurgents and those in the way of establishing peace here. On a daily basis they dodge snipers bullets, car bombs hidden explosives, suicide bombers in the form of men, women and children. Unfortunately sometimes they get hit and when they come to us we proudly step up to help them in every way. They come to our hospital, the 332 EMDG Balad Iraq to live and if they can get to us alive we offer them a 98 percent chance of going home alive. We do not tire of caring for them and when necessary we work days with little sleep, but surprising with less fatigue than we have ever experienced in the past. There is no such thing as an 8 or even 12 hour work day for the surgeons. The next time you see a soldier in Desert fatigues smile, and shake their hand. They are doing what our government has asked them to do and they do it very well—the tip of the spear.*

*Love, Jay*

## Society of Government Service Urologists (SGSU) Newsletter Article

After I had been here for about forty days, I wrote this article for the Society of Government Service Urologists newsletter.

*This month we lost the Army's 10th Combat Support Hospital (CSH), Baghdad urologist Ed Paquette to a basketball injury that required his return to the U.S. for surgery. He is missed in Baghdad and many of his patients are now being sent to Balad, making my clinics very busy. I hope that Ed is doing well and will be able to return to all of the sport activities he enjoys. I know that the 10 CSH appreciated his service and were sad to send him home.*

*Today is Sunday. I went to the dining facility for lunch. There are two big screen TVs located in opposite ends of the dining hall. It was busy and there were only a few open seats except, at the table near the big screen re-playing the weekend political talk shows. I noticed that only two people were sitting at that long table closest to the TV and both with their backs to the screen. Recently the Stars and Stripes newspaper published an article detailing a fresh report from the DOD about our influence in Iraq. The report indicated that we had made little or no progress in restoring basic services to the Iraqi people such as electricity, water, or sewer nor had we made any progress in stopping the number of insurgent attacks and IED blasts in the last 2 years. There are many complicated political reasons for these facts.*

*The release of this report by the Department of Defense received a lot of national attention and as a result I personally received some e-mail correspondence asking about the soldier's thoughts on how the war was going. In fact, I had not really given it much thought, and as I asked some of the combat forces about their opinion, I realized that they had not given it much thought either. There is certainly adequate access to TV, papers and internet but I have not been staying "current" on all of the national issues, including the politics of* the war in Iraq. There is something very different about actually being in the war in Iraq that changes your priorities. For those of us serving here, it is not about debates, roundtable discussions, should we or shouldn't we, and the second guess opinions of weekend talk show pundits. All of those questions are basically irrelevant now for those of us here. Of course these debates need to continue and will have great impact in the future, but we have immediate concerns about the war in Iraq that deal with realities, instead of the probabilities and possibilities for the future of Iraq and any other country for that matter.

The reality of the war in Iraq gets transported to the 332 EMDG in Balad day and night in the bundles of blankets containing U.S. and Coalition Military, Iraqi military, police and many Iraqi civilians, whose best efforts to restore some semblance of 'normalcy' to the their lives have been interrupted by the realities of war. We see an average of six improvised explosive devise and four gunshot wounds each day. Occasionally those brought to see us are well recognized celebrity faces, who have suffered the same reality as thousands of others who are essentially unknown to the rest of the world, but impacted the same way. The rare, celebrity touching events brings the media focus back to the palpable dangers of war, but only for a day or two. On a daily basis I talk to the men and women at the tip of the spear poked into Iraq. I promise you that the young infantry, cavalry or Marine ground soldier is not thinking much about the politics of the war, but is thinking every minute about doing his or her job, protecting their battle buddies, protecting themselves and going home intact and alive. Doing what the soldiers do here in Iraq is simply their job. It is not about the politics of the war and whether or not they agree with the political opinions about the war. Instead, they performing tasks that they have been trained to do and building upon that foundation to do things that they never trained to do. The U.S. military forces are here to carry out a mission the United States President and Congress decided they should do. For them, and for us, deployment is not about the politics of the war, but an obligation as members of the armed forces. The main difference—this is not an exercise and the hazards are real and the consequences tangible. We recently cared for a soldier who has lived through 11 IED blasts in the past 10 months and was anxious to get treated and back to his unit to finish his tour. He begged not to be returned the States or Germany and was looking forward to coming back in about a year for his 3rd tour. This is the spirit of the vast majority of patients in our hospital. That same day we cared for a soldier who suffered a fatal injury on the very last patrol of his 12 month tour of duty.

As I come to the completion of my active duty service, I am humbled by the scenes of determination, courage and sacrifice that I have witnessed here in Iraq. Never have I been more proud to be serving in the armed forces and never have I been more impressed with the capabilities and fortitude of the young U.S. fighting men and women. I know that few military physicians want to deploy to Iraq, but the fact is they need us here to support the forces in ways that we have never supported them in the States and as long as we *wear the uniforms it is our obligation to come here and support them even if it is not pleasant and convenient for our family, academic or professional lives. It is also not convenient or pleasant to suffer a gunshot wound to the scrotum or kidney. Nor is it convenient to have your bladder ruptured and your urethra injured in a Humvee rollover. It is not convenient to drop a kidney 4 mm stone into your ureter in the middle of a sniper mission with 3 other Navy SEALS that brings a 3 week mission to a sudden stop. Once you get here it takes only several trauma patients to realize that what was an obligation and inconvenience, has suddenly become an honor and you soon realize that this is the most significant work you will ever do as a physician and surgeon in uniform.*

*Today during the Sunday lunch hours, the dining faculty was busier than usual, but I saw a seat near the other big screen TV in the back, airing coverage of the winter Olympic Games, and took the last seat facing the screen.*

*Jay T. Bishoff*
*LT COL, USAF, MC*
*332 EMDG Baghdad Iraq*

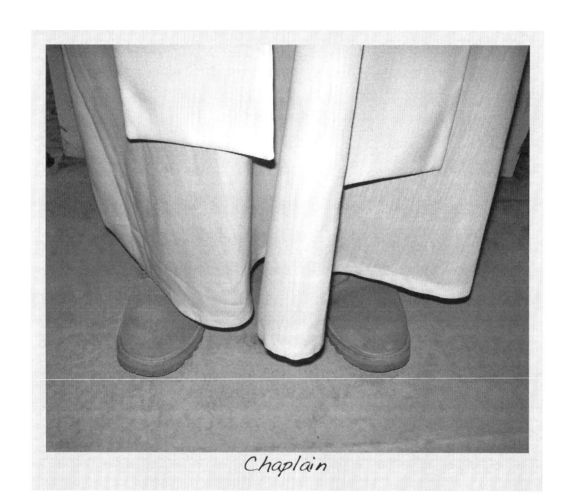

Chaplain

# Chapter 4

———

# THANK GOD FOR HIS TENDER MERCIES

1/26/06

Several months prior to my deployment, I heard a powerful sermon developed from two scriptures: "The Lord is good to all: and his tender mercies are over all his works."[1] The other scripture was "I will show unto you that the tender mercies of the Lord are over all those whom he hath chosen, because of their faith, to make them mighty even unto the power of deliverance."[2,3] The sermon had a great impact upon me and I think of it often as a way to remind me of subtle, positive affirmations or tender mercies that come to all of us from time to time, especially when I am discouraged and losing hope.

A young man, age sixteen, was seen by the urologist in our clinic five months ago for a condition where the urinary hole in his penis came out at the top of his scrotum. In addition, his penis was severely bent or curved. The condition is called penoscrotal hypospadias. In the United States this condition would commonly be corrected by the age of two. Through the use of a translator, his father explained that throughout his son's life the other children in his village had made fun of him for not being like the rest of the boys. After Dr. Lynch left to return home, the boy's case was approved by the humanitarian care committee, giving him permission to come to our hospital for surgical correction.

We scheduled him for surgery, and with the assistance of our plastic surgeon, we spent four hours straightening his penis and performing the first stage to relocate the opening to the tip of his penis. The surgery went well. He was discharged the next day, and then four months later the second stage was performed. The patient refused all pain medication and was visibly very happy to have started the process toward being like the other boys in his village. On the day his father came to pick him up, I had been somewhat discouraged about whether we were making any difference in the lives of the Iraqi people. As I walked past the Iraqi ward, I was taken aback by the bandages, external bone fixaters, amputations, and disfigured faces of Iraqi police, military and civilians. I wondered if we were really helping these people, or if we made their lives worse by coming here.

———

1　Psalm 145:9
2　I Nephi 1:20
3　"The Tender Mercies of the Lord" Elder David A Bednar, of the Quorum of the Twelve Apostles, Ensign, May 2005

Figure 7. Iraqi patient with his mother and father.

It was then that I saw the boy's father, with his distinguished dark features and striking gray beard, coming toward me. He grabbed me and kissed me. With big tears in his eyes he explained, through a translator, how he had tried unsuccessfully the past fifteen years to get his only son "fixed." And now, the Americans had come to Iraq, freed the country from Saddam and done for his family what the Iraqi doctors would not or could not do.

For me, it was one of those "tender mercies" the Lord sends to let us know we are doing the right thing.

Iraqi Interpreter

————

# Chapter 5

# IRAQ HAS ITS OWN WAR HEROES

This story is about one of our patients. He was injured around Christmas time before we arrived. He displayed courage, determination and hope, despite his serious injuries, that we did not see in most of the other Iraqi patients. I had the privilege of operating on this Iraqi army soldier and caring for him on a daily basis for about forty days. It was only after he left for rehabilitation in the States that I found this article in the *Washington Times* detailing his personal experience with the war.

INJURED SOLDIER 'A BEACON OF HOPE'
By Maya Alleruzzo
THE WASHINGTON TIMES
January 25, 2006
(Reprinted with permission)

Bagdad AIR BASE, Iraq – The powerful legs that carried him through battle lay stretched before him, motionless underneath a blanket. The broad shoulders and bulging forearms that once easily carried an 80-pound machine gun lay limp at his sides. Somewhere in Iraq, those who tried to kill him wait to finish the job.

Capt. Furat, 28, struggles to sort out a life that was shattered Christmas Day in an ambush by gun-men disguised as Iraqi soldiers while he was visiting his family.

His wounds are slowly beginning to heal. The surgical staples holding his abdomen together are gone.

He somehow survived the destruction of 12 bullets, but one of them cut through his spinal cord, leaving him paralyzed from the waist down.

"I am a dream. My future is very dark. These are the legs of Captain Furat," he said.

Other wounds include a bullet-shattered arm. They will heal but the paralysis is permanent. His family and doctors are searching for a solution to the next hurdle.

Normally, once an Iraqi patient is stable, he is transferred to a local hospital for follow-up care. But the news of Capt. Furat's survival traveled quickly through Muqdadiyah.

His family fears the killers will finish the job when he leaves this heavily guarded American base for a local hospital protected only by a few Iraqi policemen.

Col. Elisha Powell, commander of the 332nd Expeditionary Medical Group that runs the hospital, said Capt. Furat will stay there until he recovers.

The Air Force Theater Hospital in Bagdad is the busiest field hospital in Iraq. It consists of a sea of tents that house everything from state-of-the art operating rooms to patient wards with up to 10 beds per tent.

## 96 percent survive

"If you come here alive, you have a 96 percent chance of leaving here alive," said Col. Powell.

Americans typically are stabilized and flown to Landstuhl Regional Medical Facility in Germany for follow-up treatment, then on to the United States.

Though 70 percent of patients here are Americans, the hospital also treats Iraqi security forces and civilians.

Iraqis like Capt. Furat are usually transferred to Iraqi hospitals or sent home when they are well enough.

Now that he is stable, he will need to learn to use his arms and upper body to lift himself and use a wheelchair. But before that can happen, his right arm must heal, and that could take up to eight months.

"He doesn't fit the typical patient that we usually see," said Lt. Col. Jim Keeney, one of the hospital's orthopedic surgeons.

## He fought the enemy

A decorated officer with the 2nd Battalion of the 2nd Brigade of the 5th Iraqi Army Division – also known as the Tiger Battalion – based at Camp Falloc, 54 miles northeast of Baghdad, Capt. Furat loves Iraq and fought its enemies with a passion that won praise from American and Iraqi troops.

U.S. soldiers of Task Force 1-30 who worked with Capt. Furat often called him "Rambo"; he could wield an 80-pound machine gun and belts of ammunition as if carrying an Uzi.

"To me he is a superhero," said 1st Lt. John Newton of Hague, Va., from the 1st Battalion of the 30th Infantry Regiment of the 3rd Infantry Division, who wept at Capt. Furat's bedside hours after the attack.

"He was fearless under fire," said Lt. Col. Roger Cloutier, commander of Task Force 1-30, from Fort Benning, Ga.

## Few visits home

Capt. Furat, who uses only his given name because of continued threats to his family, rarely visited home for the same reason. When not on patrol or other missions, he stayed on base while other soldiers saw their families for brief periods.

His commander, Col. Theya Abd Ismael Al-Tamimmi, warned him not to go home. But his family wanted to see him, and on the weekend of Dec.23, he went.

"He was out on vacation with no security and they got him," said Col. Cloutier, whose men share a home base with the Tiger Battalion. "He was a wanted man."

Capt. Furat brought along Sgt. Hussein, 21, a fellow soldier in the Dali Abbas Company of the Tiger Battalion. As they drove back to base, a red Opel station wagon blocked their path. Three masked gunmen in Iraqi Army uniforms opened fire.

## One attacker killed

At first, Capt. Furat did not shoot back because of the uniforms. He killed one of his attackers. Three civilians caught in the crossfire also died and Capt. Furat and Sgt. Hussein were severely wounded Sgt. Hussein with nine bullets to his leg and arm. Capt. Furat took 12 shots.

They were taken to the American field hospital at nearby Base Normandy and then by helicopter to the Air Force Hospital for surgery. As doctors worked to save their lives, they managed to give enough information for Iraqi soldiers to raid the ambush site and arrest two men involved in the attack.

On the operating table, a damaged kidney was removed from Capt. Furat and a metal plate was used to repair his right forearm, hit by a bullet. A computer-assisted-tomography scan revealed how much more damage one of the bullets did.

"We knew at the time it had crossed through his spinal cord," said Maj. Alan Murdock. "Once they're cut, nerves don't usually regenerate."

For two days, Capt. Furat would be under heavy sedation and connected to a ventilator.

Soon, the doctors would have to tell him the news.

## Devastating word

"I was very straightforward with him about what to expect: That he'd be in a wheelchair," said Maj. Jeffrey McNeil, a cardiothoracic surgeon.

"It's kind of like a professional athlete having a career-ending injury," said Lt. Col. Jim Keeney, an orthopedic surgeon at Balad. "He is going to be much more functional but it's going to be a setback."

For Capt. Furat, the news was devastating. On some days, he just wept. On other days, he burned with rage.

"I love Iraq," he said in fluent English, which he learned in college during the presidency of Saddam Hussein. "I worked all over Iraq and liked all the soldiers I worked with. I loved my body. I loved

Jay T. Bishoff MD

all the civilians I helped, but I don't think all the civilians loved me. I was a brave soldier. I helped anybody – men, women, children.

## Nobody helped

"But when Ali Baba shot me, and when I lay there in the street and couldn't move, nobody helped me. Why? Capt. Furat is dead because Capt. Furat is weak. Nobody on the street helped him."

Capt. Furat enlisted in the Iraqi Army when he was 18, and was stationed in Baghdad and Mosul. He rose through the ranks, attended Army College and was part of an elite special forces unit.

When American soldiers entered Baghdad in April 2003, Capt. Furat was in the capital with the Al Qanata Brigade.

"I told my platoon, 'hey, don't move,'? he recalled. "I saw the U.S. Army coming toward us. My platoon shot at them with their AK-47s. They were very noble.

"I couldn't kill anyone. [The Americans] had big weapons, but all I had was a pistol and an AK-47."

## Stranger took him in

He took a bullet in the leg during the battle and somehow managed to escape amid the confusion, taking shelter in a stranger's house.

"He cut off my uniform and gave me pajamas," Capt. Furat recalled. "He took my weapon and pistol and ID and went to the garden and buried them in the earth.

"I was afraid the U.S. Army would come in the house. I saw through the window the Army in the street."

He stayed there five days, then his host drove him to his family's home in Diyala province, not far from base.

"My father thought I was dead because a soldier came to the house and said he saw me get shot by the Americans.

31

## U.S. sought officers

"When I knocked on the door, my father saw me and he couldn't believe it was me. I hugged him to my chest and wept."

Capt. Furat stayed with his family in Muqdadiyah for about a year.

"I had no work, no dreams. I just sat in the house."

Then he heard through a friend that American troops at nearby Base Falloc, the former site of an Iraqi Army division, were looking for former Iraqi officers to begin building the new army. He joined, and has since worked with six or seven different groups of American soldiers.

"I was with the last group for three or four months before Ali Baba shot me," he says. "I'd go with them anywhere. I trust them, and they trust me. Now I am sad. This life was very good. I worked with kings, not soldiers. But I can't move with them."

## Inspiration to others

"My dream is just to stand up with my legs," he said. "When I can stand up with my legs, just tell me and I'll go anywhere – Iraq, Afghanistan, Iran – just tell me."

As Capt. Furat works through the physical and emotional trauma of his tragedy, those on the hospital staff see an opportunity for the disabled soldier.

"He could be a beacon of hope for all the handicapped people in Iraq," said Col. Powell.

"He could be a champion, a great one. There are going to be thousands of disabled people here, maybe more. There's nothing keeping him from doing anything. We just want him to reach his full potential."

Figure 8. Capt. Furat spent months in the 332<sup>nd</sup> hospital while his wounds healed. Shown here with Omar, a young Iraqi who suffered significant burns. Capt. Furat was often found comforting young Iraqi patients and motivating older Iraqi soldiers to return to duty.

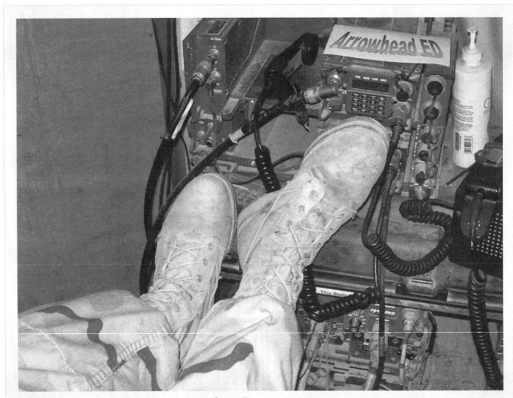

ER Technician

Chapter 6

_____

# WAIT, WHAT IS THE DATE ON THAT SCAN?

2/1/06

Dr. Omar, from Balad, came to the hospital on Saturdays to discuss transfers for Iraqi patients to the Balad Medical City Hospital and to bring cases for us to review. After several months he did not come back. Because of death threats to his family he had fled to Jordan. On this particular day he came to the urology office specifically to see me. He held a big bag of x-ray films all rolled up. He reached in and handed me one page with twelve slices from a CT scan.

"This patient is a three year-old girl with a kidney tumor," he started.

I looked at the scan and saw not just a tumor but a mass filling her entire left abdomen, from her ribs to her pelvis, and growing across midline. There was extensive necrosis in the center.

"Well, of course, we can help her," I said as I looked at the date on the CT scan in the left hand corner with all of the other data. I did a double-take because the scan was almost a year old. The enormous tumor was still intact in her tiny body. The question rushed through my mind and straight out my mouth, "Why does she still have the tumor a year after a scan like this?"

Dr. Omar saw the shock on my face, "This is Iraq and we are at war. We all do what we can."

I saw her three weeks later in clinic. Her mother tried to get her to me earlier but was denied entrance at the gate. The next week her sister was also denied access. Finally, three weeks later, another sister was able to enter. She held a precious three year-old toddler, who lay quietly sleeping in her arms.

"Please," she managed to say. "Please."

I smiled and nodded. I sent her to get a CT scan from head to toe. There were golf-ball size metastatic lesions filling her lungs on both sides, and the mass growing from her kidney was much larger, occupying essentially her entire abdomen. I could not help her. No one could help her. With the aid of an interrupter and with tears in my eyes I explained that there was nothing anyone could do to treat her. It was simply too late. Her aunt understood and asked if there was anything I could do to ease the little child's pain. There was something I could do for her. It was not much, and certainly not enough in my mind. I went to the pharmacy and picked up several bottles of Tylenol with codeine elixir, handed it to her aunt, wiped away several tears and went back to the urology clinic. There was nothing else I could do. Patients were waiting.

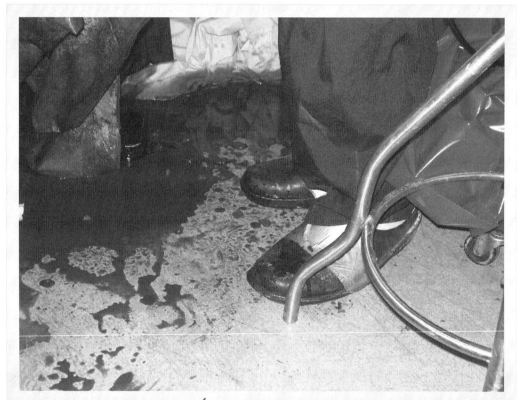

*Neurosurgeon*

Chapter 7

———

# AFTER A YEAR IN IRAQ, ONE LAST PATROL

2/17/06

On an average day in Iraq there are fifty IEDs discovered. Some are disarmed, but some go off. Today there was a call for help to unload choppers, which usually means many casualties. An IED had exploded in the city of Balad, and there were four patients with head injuries. One large, tattooed Marine seemed to be worse off than the other three so he went to the scanner first. There was a large hematoma in the left hemisphere of his brain. He was taken immediately to the OR for removal of his skull to allow the blood clot to be removed and to allow his brain to swell without being restricted by the bony limits of his skull.

The procedure for Americans who require head surgery is to throw the skull cap away. Later, if the patient survives, a replacement skull cap is manufactured from synthetic materials using the other side as a model. The new cap is placed under the skin and then used to cover the brain to restore a more normal look to the head. For Iraqis, the skull cap is placed under the skin of the abdominal wall at the time of the initial brain exploration and if needed later, retrieved and replaced in the original position.

So varied and extensive were this Marine's wounds that it took a whole team of specialists to operate on him. Neurosurgeons worked to clear the blood out from under the skull and to stop the bleeding caused from an embedded piece of the IED. An ophthalmologist worked to salvage his badly damaged eye. General surgeons opened his abdomen to remove perforated loops of intestine. I worked to fix the blast effects to his scrotum and testis. Several hours later he was in the ICU being prepared for a trip to Germany for more surgery, and then a trip to Walter Reed Army Medical Center.

It was late, and before leaving the hospital I went back to check my e-mail. There was a message from our commander, Colonel Taylor, forwarded from the injured soldier's commander. It was addressed to all the surgeons at the hospital, inquiring about the status of his Marine. The commander wrote, "I have received word that Corporal Hansen is seriously injured. I need to know his status. He has been here for one year. He was on his last patrol tonight and is scheduled to go home tomorrow."

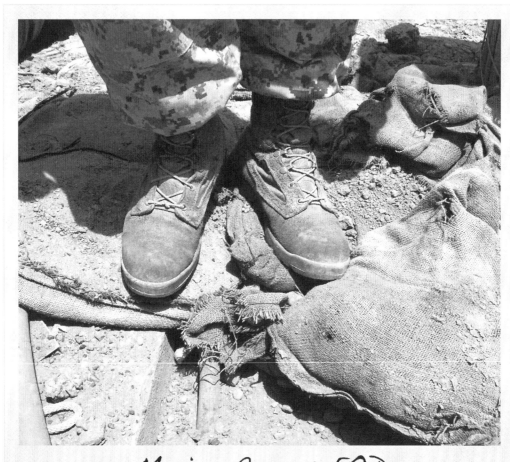

Marine Corps EOD

# Chapter 8

-----

# WHO CAN YOU TRUST?

2/18/06

Today I saw Staff Sergeant McBride, who had been stationed outside the city of Ramadi, one of the most dangerous cities in Iraq at the present time. At the age of twenty-five he is one of the older men in his platoon. He is in charge of about fifteen others he calls "my boys" because they are all about nineteen years old. He and his boys patrol three days in a row, and then have one day off to clean their gear and rest. He was in the hospital with an open nose fracture that had been fixed, but he had a penile lesion he wanted checked before he went back to work.

His nose had been broken in an IED explosion in which no one else was injured. He was anxious to get back to his boys, who kept e-mailing him that they did not feel safe going on patrol without him. Two weeks earlier he had been out with his boys winning the hearts and minds of the Iraqis by distributing candy and school supplies, and playing soccer, as well as you can play soccer, wearing full body-armor and your weapon in the ready position. He and his boys had been playing with the same group of kids for several weeks and knew many of their names. On a Tuesday, they talked to the kids in the village, gave them gum and then loaded up in three Humvees to return to camp. Normally in a small village, if something bad is going to happen, the children scatter or avoid the area, usually because their parents have warned them about a planted IED or other possible ambush attack.

On that Tuesday, the children did not scatter but lingered to say goodbye to the soldiers, who thought they were making progress in winning the hearts and minds of the people. SSgt McBride was in the front car and had just turned to see if all of his boys were loaded. A young Iraqi boy standing in the crowd of other kids, next to the third vehicle, blew himself up, killing six Iraqi kids and two of McBride's boys.

H-60 Mechanic

# Chapter 9

---

# SOMEONE IS ON FIRE

2/19/06

I share a clinic with three other military services in a tent adjacent to the ER but not actually attached to the hospital. Tonight I was in the clinic finishing up some e-mail letters when I heard one chopper, then another, and then a third followed by yet one more. The helipad only holds four choppers. Because of the sudden traffic, I knew something was up so I hustled and logged off the computer. The air had the unmistakable smell of burning flesh, and there was suddenly a lot of activity outside the tent on the way to the ER. The stench and commotion were intense.

I ran to help put out what I thought was surely a fire in the ER, but as I left the clinic, the ER didn't appear to be in flames. Then I caught a glimpse of two medics struggling to carry a large person through the ER doors. The patient wasn't on a NATO cot with wheels, which is the usual method of transporting the wounded. The chopper that was sitting in the rocks off to the side of the landing pad hovered just above the ground for a few seconds, and then abruptly faded into the black night sky. Two medics were firmly holding the patient under his arms while two others were trying to carry his legs with some difficulty due to his size and the burned flesh that kept slipping off in their hands. The acrid smell was so strong it seemed strange that I could not see flames or at least some smoke.

Only the man's large shoulders offered some clues to his race and history. On his left shoulder were brilliantly colored tattoos, including the Marine Corps insignia. On the right was a red dragon whose tail disappeared into his black charred forearm and fingers. Much of the skin was had been burned off by the fire, exposing bones and strands of tissue. His boots, legs and abdomen were black and deeply burned. His pupils were fixed and dilated. No one in the clinic had seen someone so badly burned. Even after the code was called and the patient was pronounced dead, we all lingered, paralyzed really, frozen by the sight of something so horrific that it actually overshadowed all the horror we'd previously experienced. We were trying not to look into each others faces. In our minds we were trying to picture, yet not really wanting to, how a human could be so badly burned.

Suddenly we were jolted out of our mutual trance by a second lieutenant nurse yelling, "This is no damn dog and pony show!"

He grabbed a blanket throwing it over the remains of one of America's finest. Then he suddenly realized that this man was much larger than one blanket could cover, so he grabbed another and covered the honorable soldier to protect his dignity as he rolled him back to the morgue.

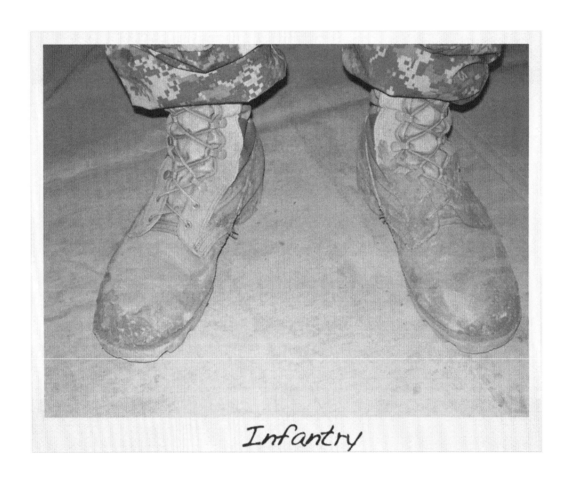

Infantry

# Chapter 10

_____

# SOMEWHERE BETWEEN THE END AND THE TIP OF THE SPEAR

2/20/06

The expression "the tip of the spear" refers to those who are fighting on the front lines, the ground forces like the infantry, cavalry, and Marines. Most of the time surgeons believe they are at the tip of everything. It only takes a few days of being in Iraq to realize the tip is where the nineteen- and twenty-year-old soldiers are, and we support personnel are somewhere in the shaft. Ours is an important role too, but it is subordinate and supportive to the tip of the spear.

When I see individuals from the front, they are usually able to speak as opposed to being intubated and unconscious. After I treat them I usually ask them, "What is the wildest thing you have seen?"

Today a young but capable Army soldier from the 101st Airborne Division told me that the wildest thing he had seen happened the previous week. He was riding in an armored vehicle with thick bullet-proof windows when a young man on a moped suddenly pulled up near the vehicle. He continued riding along side for some distance, all the while yelling and gesturing in a hostile manner. Suddenly, he veered right up against the bus and blew himself up in a terrible explosion. The armored car screeched to a stop and everyone clamored out, safe, but dazed and with ears still ringing.

"It took us an hour to clean the kid off that car, Doc," was all he said.

Patient Admit & Disposition

# Chapter 11

———

# HEY DOC, YOU GOT ANYTHING FOR THAT?

2/21/06

On Tuesday, all of the clinics see Iraqis who have been injured in the war. Some are police, others military, and unfortunately many are civilians. It takes them hours to get to the base, and then it takes more hours to process through the gate. It usually takes them until early afternoon to arrive. That leaves very little time to process them through the hospital and treat them. Labs and films usually need to be taken, and they all need translators, but only four are available. Also, while in the hospital, they have to have a U.S. escort, which means my tech or I need to be with them at all times, including escorting them to labs, radiology, or anywhere else. Then the Iraqis are required to be on a bus back to the front gate by 1600. If they're late, they have to be boarded in the hospital for the night.

Today all of the clinics were packed with Iraqi nationals, and there was simply not enough time to process them all through labs, radiology, and clinics. They were upset, and we were tired, but finally the magic hour came, and all the patients shuffled, hobbled, ran, or were carried back to the bus, including all twelve of the patients from my clinic. We had somehow managed to get them all back to the front gate on time. I thought I finally had a minute to relax.

Wrong! A frenzied knock on the door quickly brought me back to reality—Iraq reality! I opened the door and in stepped an infantry trooper all decked out in body armor, day bag, and weapon. He was in desperate need of a urologist to help him with testis pain. Fortunately, he only had a simple infection and was quickly reassured and appropriately treated.

This gave me the opportunity to ask him my favorite question as we walked to the pharmacy to get Motrin and antibiotics: "What is the wildest thing you have seen?"

"Well," he started. "I guess, technically, this whole week has been wild. We have been busy chasing a bunch of snipers in Ramadi. On Sunday one of them shot our first sergeant in the left knee. He was squatting, and the round hit him on the front of the knee, went right through the long part of his thigh bone, and then blew right out the back of his butt. That was Sunday!

"Then on Monday, the first sergeant from our other company was shot in the left shoulder just above the edge of his body armor—a damn-near perfect shot. I think they are both going to be out for about a year. Apparently the snipers can see our rank markings from the distance, so we had to strip them off our uniforms.

"Tuesday we were on patrol when some mortars started zeroing-in on our position. We scrambled across a narrow board bridge that goes across a city sewer stream so we could take cover in a field. Just as I got on the board, a mortar landed close and knocked me into the sewer stream. With all my gear I sunk right up to my chin. Two of my guys grabbed me just before my head went under, but then small-arms fire started hitting all around us, rounds even bouncing off our helmets and body armor. No serious injures though.

"After they pulled me out of the sewer, we saw some people on the roof of a building across from us, so we started shooting at them. Our radios rang out telling us to knock it off—it was our other company. They had climbed to the roof of the building to see where the mortars were coming from so they could call in air support. Since they had secured the building and were in a much better position than we were in the open field, we ran back across the sewer towards the building. Before we reached the building a car with three insurgents came by shooting at us with AK-47s. We returned fire hitting the driver who crashed into the sewer stream just as a Cobra helicopter arrived and blew the car into a hundred pieces.

"So, Doc, my whole week has been wild. I got dumped into a sewer and had to work all day with those stinkin' clothes on. But now that I think about it, I have not taken a crap all week. Got anything for that?"

Command Sergeant Major

# Chapter 12

———

# IED

**2/23/06**

This morning was quiet and average. Patients in the ICU were ready for transfer to the ward or for air evac to Germany. Patients ready to be moved from the self-care ward were waiting for a ride back to their unit by plane or helicopter. Most people here don't drive on the roads because it is too dangerous.

In the early afternoon there was a call to help incoming patients in the ER. Two Black Hawk helicopters had landed and unloaded five patients. All had been injured by an IED in a city about ten miles away. One had a critical injury to the right lower leg and went immediately to the OR for fasciotomy, a procedure in which the skin and underlying fascia is widely opened to allow the damaged tissue to swell without occluding the arteries and veins in the leg.

Another patient had five or six penetrating soft tissue wounds to the right leg, left knee, face, and scrotum. I took him to the OR to explore the scrotum. Now the scrotum is a muscle sac covered in skin and can expand to large proportions. During an IED blast the scrotum expands and then contracts in a millisecond. During expansion there is often a small tear or abrasion resulting as it rapidly inflates, expands, and then deflates.

The testicle itself has a dense covering called the tunica. It cannot expand and contract like the muscular scrotum, so if there is a small abrasion on the surface, there is usually a complete rupture on the inside. This patient appeared to have this same type of predictable blast pattern. However, as I opened the scrotum there was an expected rupture of the testis, but something hard in the center. I dug into the contents of the testis and pulled out a one-by-two-centimeter piece of bone. I was able to save half of the testis.

The orthopedic surgeons working on the same patient then proceeded to pull out ten pieces of bone fragments from his right calf and upper leg. Oral surgery and ENT were busy doing other things, so I pulled three bone fragments from his face and did a meticulous plastic closure of the wounds with 6-0 nylon suture. We have seen rocks, ball bearings, and now bone in IED—such is the glamour of this war.

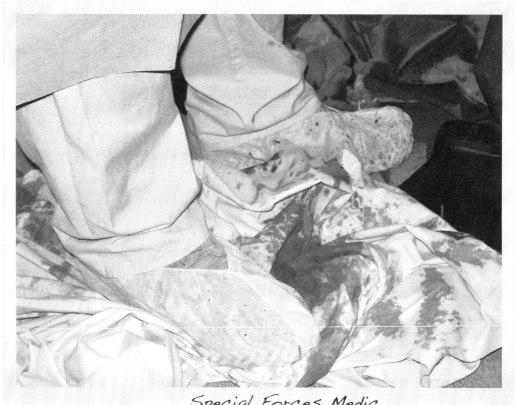

Special Forces Medic

# Chapter 13

———

# FIRE FRIENDS

2/25/06

Sergeant Stewart is an Army .50-caliber sniper currently working with other Special Forces. He talks about his job like a banker talks about closing a loan. Sometimes it takes him three weeks to "close the loan." That seems like a lot of time in preparation, but all the "documents" have to be in a very particular order. You could say things have to line up just right.

Several weeks ago Stewart and his squad were working with another squad trying to get things lined up right to close a loan on a Chechen sniper who had been closing loans on our forces. In the middle of a day's work in the city of Ramadi, the squads, four men each, became entangled in a very difficult situation involving increasingly accurate mortar attacks and rifle fire. They were pinned down and each had an injured man. As Stewart looked at the others, he feared that their luck had run out, and they would likely die.

As a last resort they implemented their bail-out procedure. This involved using a secure radio frequency (which he was not interested in talking about) to call for "fire friends," (which he was anxious to talk about because it seemed to him they had saved his life.) Apparently, when small sniper squads are in trouble they call in fire friends, other Special Forces units in the area, to come rescue them. They made the call and waited. Minutes later a white Mercedes rounded a corner driving down the middle of the street between the squads and the building drawing all enemy fire against them. Some one in the Mercedes stuck an M-16 out of the sun-roof and sprayed a long burst of fire in a circle of fire that continued until the car stopped. Then five heavily armed soldiers jumped out laying down a constant barrage of fire directed towards the windows, which moments earlier were full of insurgent rifles, rockets and mortars.

Fire Friends had arrived. One of them pulled a shoulder-fired rocket from the trunk and shot it into the window that seemed to be the busiest. As the middle floor of the building exploded they rushed inside throwing shock grenades, fragmentation grenades and delivering almost non-stop fire until they declared the building secured. Fire friends—we would all be lucky to have one or two.

However, that is not the end of this story. I was a bit concerned about the truth of this story, so I coaxed Stewart into telling it to his nurse and one of the other surgeons. Each time it was exactly the same. After he was discharged from the hospital, we had several Special Forces or other coalition forces medics in the hospital OR and the ER brushing up on their training. One day they were operating with me, so I told them Sergeant Stewart's story. But I said the city was Tikrit, and I changed Stewart's name (even though it was a fake name he had given to us). They both indicated that the story was not likely to be true because "grenades are not used in that way to clear buildings" and the "weapons and tactics sounded all wrong."

"And I have been to all of the bases in Iraq with Special Forces," said one of the medics, "and the only place we had a white up-armored Mercedes and Army snipers working with Seals was several months ago in Ramadi."

I am still not sure if this was a true story, but I certainly like the idea of fire friends. We would all be lucky to have a few.

50 Cal Sniper

# Chapter 14

———

# BIRTHDAY IN IRAQ

2/26/2006

My forty-fourth birthday came and went today. It seemed like just another day in Iraq except with presents. I opened the two presents I had been saving. One was a wonderful box from my wife Kris, and the other was from the Young Women's group from our church at the Stone Oak Ward. There were no cards or letters from my kids however, which caused me to ponder about my relationship with them, and my success or failure as a father.

Because it was my birthday, we celebrated by giving out a lot of candy to soldiers in for clinic visits. We have a candy closet in the clinic, which we keep loaded with goodies—almost everything that is good to eat from the States—to brighten the lives of our patients. After a clinic visit, we point to the storage cabinet in the office and ask them to help themselves. Their eyes brighten as they survey our stash of Swedish fish, potatoes chips, beef jerky, peanut butter, chocolate, Peeps, nuts, and gum. They would apologetically take just a few items, and then Sergeant Sechler and I would have to encourage them to take more. We knew that when most of them would go back to their units there would be some friend to share with, someone who was covering their shifts and patrols while they were at the hospital, and new supplies arrived from the states almost every day.

For my birthday, I celebrated by sleeping in until 1000 hours. I was surprised to have slept that long, but was tired from some recent late nights and early morning calls over the past several days. I was happy to hear one of the surgeons say, "It is getting harder and harder for me to stay up late, operate and still function the next day. When I was in my thirties, it was not a problem. But now at forty I can't keep up."

My feelings exactly and a great reason to be in urology, I mused. For my birthday I received a new bike helmet (ordered several weeks ago), some games, a twenty-question answer ball, CDs from Kris, and a nice card and letter from my mom.

It was slow at the hospital today for most of us, but not for the general surgeons. There is usually an interesting story of the day to report, and today was no exception. Today we readmitted the army sniper who told the story about the fire friends, Sergeant Stewart, for a kidney stone. His case had been complicated by an *E. coli* infection and obstruction of his kidney from a kidney stone. After arriving at Balad, he became septic and was too ill to evacuate. His condition required a ureteral stent and a stay in the ICU for three days until he began to recover. Once the infection had cleared, we treated the stone and watched him for a week before removing the stent and returning him to duty.

Stewart gave also gave me a birthday present, the following story: He is a sniper and his weapon is the feared .50 caliber. He and his company had been monitoring and pursuing Chechen snipers working in the Ramadi area. One day they were closer than they thought to the snipers, who will sometimes take several weeks to set up a single shot to make a kill. This sniper had taken several weeks to research the location and area for the shot. He used a common technique to create a physical baffle to help silence the noise from his rifle. When baffled correctly, the muzzle blast will not be heard and the sniper's location remains undetected. In the area Stewart's squad was working, a U.S. soldier was killed by a single shot to the head, but no one had seen or heard the sniper.

A squad member saw what looked like a local Iraqi standing on top of an adjacent building with a hand held Motorola radio, perhaps a spotter hired to help alert the sniper. A chase ensued, but within minutes the spotter was captured and quickly interrogated. The spotter identified the building immediately adjacent to them as the location of the Chechen snipers. Indeed, Stewart had been correct, they were closer than expected. They quickly entered the building being careful to look for traps, explosives, and other tricks often used by snipers to secure a location. They soon discovered the vacated floor used by the sniper and found the hole in the wall from which the bullet had originated. This sniper had chipped holes in adjacent walls inside the building to create a giant funnel shape. The hole in the wall where the bullet exited the building was only six inches in diameter. Working back from the hole in the exterior wall, the sniper had created a large cone or funnel shape by chipping out sequentially larger holes in the inside walls and lining the path with debris and lumber all the way back to where the sniper had a comfortable arm rest. The discharge of the rifle had been muffled away from the exit hole, essentially creating a silent, and in this case, lethal shot.

On the very day of this incident, the U.S. squad was trying to lure the sniper to take a shot at a decoy mannequin head and helmet, which they had attached by rubber cords to stand up in the gun turret and move with some human-like features. If they can find out the direction of the shot they have a chance to take out the sniper. Unfortunately the Chechen sniper did not take the bait, but instead waited and took a shot with real consequences. Then he disappeared into the city streets wearing local dress with his rifle dissembled and concealed under his man dress or in a plain bag. He was gone by the time Stewart's squad secured the building.

Today Stewart was almost 100 percent recovered, so I had his stent removed and sent him back to the hunt.

Anesthesiologist

# Chapter 15

---

# MORMONS IN IRAQ

2/27/06

Shortly after I arrived here, I was called to be the Latter-day Saints (LDS) Service member's group leader for the Tuskegee group. After prayerful consideration, I called Eric Olsen, from Alaska, and Jay Metcalfe, from Hawaii, to be my assistants. They are both holding the office of Elder in our church and neither had served in a church leadership position before. I am sure the Lord directed me to choose them for this reason.

Yesterday it was Metcalfe's turn to conduct, and as a result it was his responsibility to choose the music. We were all a little surprised, and he a little embarrassed, when he unwittingly chose the closing hymn, "Oh Come All Ye Faithful." When we started singing, he suddenly realized that is was very much a traditional Christmas song and we were more than a few months away from Christmas. Still, we sang it joyfully, and it just felt good!

Figure 9. Lt Col Jay Bishoff, Latter-day Saints (LDS) Service member's group leader for the Tuskegee group standing outside the Chaplain's office at the Tuskegee Chapel in Balad, Iraq.

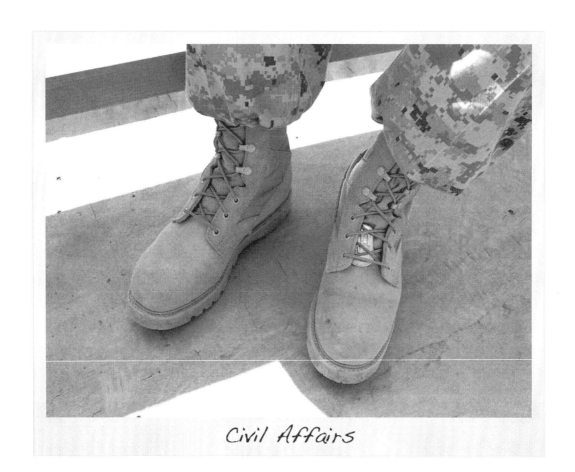

Civil Affairs

# Chapter 16

---

# OH, THOSE MORTARS WON'T STOP

2/27/06

After a good work out at the gym, I went back to the hospital to finish several chapters for the second edition of *The Atlas on Laparoscopic Urological Surgery*, a laparoscopic surgery atlas I am writing with my mentor from Johns Hopkins, Dr. Lou Kavoussi. Just as I was getting ready to leave the hospital to go to my trailer, loud sirens went off and a big voice urgently announced, "Incoming! Incoming!" The only shelter I could find was a table in the doctor's lounge area. I hastily dove for cover there, just as a deafening explosion and ground-shaking concussion rocked the hospital. This was soon followed by another loud but less violent explosion a little farther away. The speaker now loudly announced, "Alarm red, alarm red," which means get your armor and get to the shelter. I scrambled back to the office just as a third mortar landed. I grabbed my gear from the office and made a mad dash for the bunker. When I turned on the light in the bunker, I realized I was alone.

It seemed that all other hospital personnel had stayed in the hospital thinking—or not—that they were protected by the vinyl tent. After about five dangerous minutes had passed, someone apparently realized that they were like sitting-ducks on an open pond and now madly scrambling for cover. The bunker eventually filled to capacity, and we all huddled safely together waiting for the all-clear signal so we could return to work. Thirty minutes later the all-clear was announced, and we trudged back to our business. The first mortar had landed near the theater, the second near housing, and the third outside the wire behind the hospital.

It struck me later, how much like daily life that little battlefront episode actually was: we all go about doing whatever it is we do, blithly thinking—or not—that we are somehow protected by the flimsly things of life.

Infantry Cook

_____

# Chapter 17

# LUCKIEST MAN IN THE HOSPITAL TODAY

2/28/06

Today a young army infantry solider was on patrol with his squad when a single shot rang out. The shot was loud to all in the squad, but even louder to this particular soldier, as it tore through his helmet, through his ear lobe and then ripped his left cheek wide open. Except for some ringing in his ears, he was left with a facial laceration. He was fine. Next to him in the ED, lay an Iraqi translator shot with a direct hit to the head. The infantry solider looked at the patient next to him and gave a big sigh of relief, closed his eyes and crossed his chest thanking God for his minor injury. He would eventually be going home with a Purple Heart and just a scar.

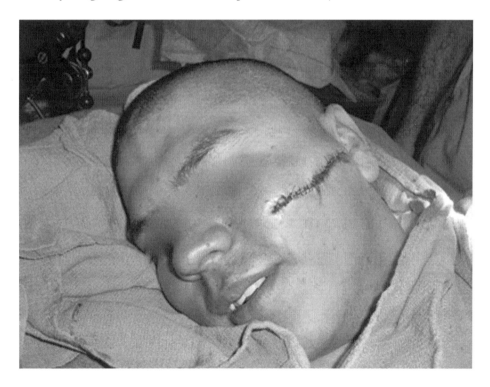

Figure 10. Soldier returned to duty after narrowly escaping what could have been a fatal gunshot wound.

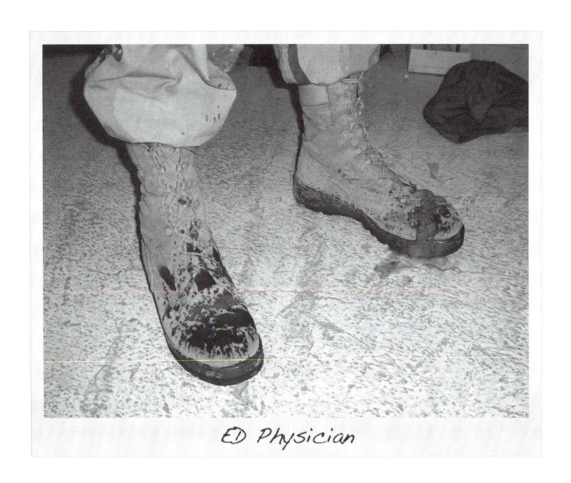

ED Physician

# Chapter 18

———

# MAYBE YOUR MOM TOLD YOU NEVER TO PLAY WITH IEDS

3/3/06

The after-action report filed by the receiving squad and shown to me by one of the Security Police read: "After several weeks of following and identifying the subject digging holes and making preparations for an apparent IED placement, he returned with a partner in a blue Fiat. After uncovering the previously created hole, they moved to the back of the car, opened the trunk and began to remove an IED. After radio clearance the individual was engaged with three 0.762 rounds. Two rounds struck the individual. He was knocked to the ground. A third round hit the roof of the blue Fiat. The individual struggled back into the car and the car sped off. We lost sight of the vehicle and radioed for visual support, but others in the area were unable to spot the vehicle. Approximately four hours later a white Caprice stopped at the FOB check point near Ramadi and deposited the previously identified and engaged individual. Positive ID was made by the surveillance team. The white Caprice attempted to leave the FOB check point. All five occupants were detained. The individual engaged was found to have serious injuries with a lot of blood loss. He was evacuated to Balad.

The ER paged and when I answered the phone I heard, "Hey Doc, you got to see this one. We have an insurgent here in the ER, and I swear to God I am serious, he was swacked in the swacker, pow, popped right in the pouch. (While I had never heard these terms or words strung together, yet I immediately knew what had happened) His penis is gone or at least I think it is gone. At best it's in pieces."

I was certainly intrigued. In the ER I saw ten or more medics, docs and nurses standing around a single gurney trying to get a look at the small dark-skinned patient with a gauze blindfold on his eyes and a large amount of blood coming out from what once was his penis and scrotum—Patient 1013.

I put on a pair of gloves and gently removed the gauze bandage loosely covering bloody remnants of testis, scrotum, and penis, inside of penis, urethra and foreskin. "Wow this is worse than it looks," I said to Shawn Varney, the ER doc of the day.

He smiled in reply, because it really did look pretty bad. It appeared that a single bullet had entered the top or anterior portion of his right thigh but directly hit his scrotum and then impacted directly into the side of his penis. The result was loss of the right testis, right hemi scrotum, base of the penis skin, splitting both the left and right corporal bodies in their entire length and inflicting damage to the left testicle. I was fairly certain I would need to amputate what was left and divert the urethra under the scrotum creating a perineal urethrostomy.

Off to the OR we went, but on the way several Special Forces, members approached me and asked about how serious the injury really was. They suggested that it would teach him a great lesson if he did not have a penis or scrotum, and since it looked pretty bad, maybe the best thing was to remove it. As I scrubbed, two techs from the OR asked me if I agreed with the suggestion to just remove everything. They also felt certain it was the best thing to do. "You know since it looks bad, and it would teach him, and hopefully a lot of other Iraqis a lesson." They kept their voices down because the place was crawling with reporters looking for a great story to send back home.

As I listened to them whispering, Dr. Paille's words from the past echoed loudly: "Bishoff, medicine and surgery trump politics every time. . . . Every time!"

Since the docs at the forward operating base (FOB) near Ramadi had already made several unsuccessful attempts to place a suprapubic bladder tube in the patient, I performed a low midline incision to explore the abdomen and rectum for injury. There were none, so I placed a suprapubic tube and closed the abdomen. Next I turned to the right testis. Essentially strands of cord structures were the only remaining pieces so I completed the orchiectomy the 0.762 round had started. The left testis was missing the lower pole, so I debrided the extruded tubules and closed the tunica. About a third of the original testicle was left, but it looked viable.

Now, to look at the penis. Could it be salvaged? The room was full of curious onlookers, and a photographer from *USA Today* snapped pictures, while a reporter from National Public Radio (NPR) asked questions and pointed his extra long, intrusive microphone in my direction. The reporter moved his microphone in closer asking for a detailed description of the injury. He then wanted to know how I felt about it, — "you know, taking care of an insurgent who was trying to kill American soldiers [and] was I simply going to remove the injured parts."

I ignored the question and intrusion, "Penorse drain, please," I asked of the scrub tech. "And you better get up about ten packs of 4-0 vicryl sutures and some 4- 0 chromic sutures. We are going to need them both."

That seemed to work to distract the NPR reporter because he moved his long microphone back out of the way.

What kind of insurgent do you become when you no longer have testis or a penis because an American soldier shot them off?  kept racing through my mind. Seemed like a perfect mix for a suicide bomber to me, assuming he ever gets out of Abu Ghraib prison. But when the prison becomes full, the guys who seemed bad eventually get bumped out to make room for the guys coming later—who seem worse. So I decided he would have to be a suicide bomber. No choice really.

"Of course, I am going to try to save his parts," I replied to the NPR reporter, who quickly shoved the microphone back in front of my face, as I tried my best to reconstruct his mangled member. The attending OR nurse just as quickly moved the microphone back out of the sterile field. "Without a penis and testis, he would be destined to be a suicide bomber!"

The reporter seemed satisfied with the answer and moved away. Just then the trauma director, Dr. Jeff Bailey, scrubbed in to assist me. I could see the large smile under his mask as news reporters persisted asking questions that seemed designed to get us to say the wrong thing.

I had placed a tourniquet earlier and now irrigated the blood away. Despite the split on both sides of the penis where the bullet had entered and then exited, the tip of the penis seemed to be well perfused and the urethra intact. But how could it be intact when all else was not? I used the cystoscope to look through the urethra. It was normal all the way into the bladder. I put a catheter that went straight down the urethra into the bladder.

Next I approximated the edges of both corporal bodies back together, somewhat like the peelings of a banana after the inside has been removed. I then reconstructed the outside segments on both sides. It was floppy to be sure, but looking more and more like a penis every minute. I closed the inside and outside of both the right and left corporal bodies and had almost no bleeding once I removed the tourniquet.

The two techs from the ER came by to check up on their recommendation, looked at the reconstructed penis and simply said, "Wow. That looks great!" and walked away.

The two Special Forces medics came soon after, looked at our progress and simply said, "Oh shit, you rebuilt it!" and walked away.

Medicine and surgery trump politics every time ... Every time!

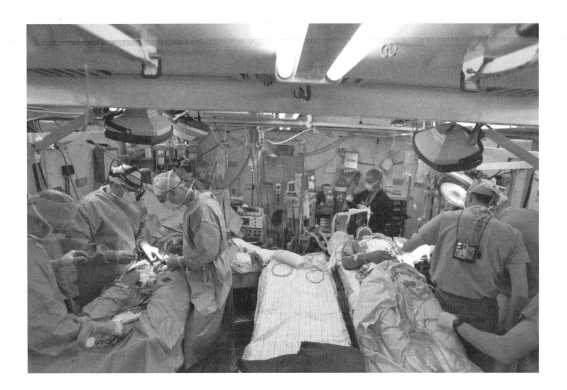

Figure 11. 332$^{nd}$ hospital's operating room #1. Two patients with severe wounds treated side-by-side. Surgeons have just finished with exploratory laparotomy for gunshot wound to the abdomen. On the left Lt Col Bishoff and Lt Col Bailey reconstruct the results of a gunshot wound to the penis.

The next problem was how to find enough skin to cover this mess. With the right testis no longer in need of a home there was some extra scrotal skin that I was able to stretch enough to create a spiral-type flap that reached to the base of the penis on the right side to close the large wound. The amazing stretching properties of the scrotum came through to help man once again. The penile shaft skin was loose enough to pull around and close the penis, with the exception of a two-centimeter area on both the top and bottom where the skin had been removed. But healthy tissue was still evident underneath.

"Wow! You could save that? Is that really Patient 1013 from the ER, who was shot in the penis?" asked one of the ER nurses who had just entered the room trying to get some follow up to take back to the rest of the department, now working on two gun shot wounds to the head. There were a lot of suture lines and flaps, but more and more it looked every bit like the penis of the insurgent who, only eight hours earlier, was healthy enough to put an IED in the ground.

"Two gun shot wounds to the head?" asked one of the reporters as his group, still searching for a story, left me and followed the nurse back to the ER. No story here. The guy was not going to lose his penis after all.

"Why did you put it all back together," complained one of the ER techs who had just come back over from the two gunshot wounds to the head to see for himself and to question my dedication to the war on terror.

"He lost his right testicle and most of the left. He will never get an erection again. So that's pretty bad, isn't it?" I asked him.

"No testicles, and no erections? Man that does suck! He is not going to like that."

USA Today Journalists

———

# Chapter 19

# DOC, I REALLY GOT TO FIND THAT NECKLACE

*3/5/06*

A trauma call to the ER came overhead, just as I was leaving to go back to my room for a quiet sunday afternoon of writing, reading, and preparation for church services. I usually stop off at the ER when there is a trauma call and I am not busy, just to see if there is any GU trauma and to see if there is anything I can do to help. Occasionally it is good to have an extra set of helpful hands to open a chest or help with an exploratory laparotomy in the OR. I am always available, but only half of the other surgeons are in the hospital at any given time.

"Hey Doc, we were just going to call you. This is one of ours this time, and he has the same problem as 1013. Swacked right in the swacker. No kidding, his testicle is right there in the breeze. Shot in the pouch. You better check it out."

"Did he really say swacked in the swacker again?" passed through my mind as he handed me a pair of gloves. Swacked in the swacker, by now everyone knew exactly what that meant.

Figure 12. Air evacuation of U.S soldier injured by an IED and small arms fire while on patrol.

A sweaty army infantryman covered with tattoos and battlefield grime looked up from his stretcher to see the expression on my face. As he tried to focus his eyes on me, dirt that had been sticking on his eyebrows fell right into his eyes, and he had to close them tightly again. I pulled back the blanket covering his groin area and was once again intrigued by what I saw there. One of the medics in the field had slapped one of the new fibrin gauze bandages right on the soldier's scrotum and exposed testis. He winced as I pulled the bandage off, but it seemed it had helped to stop most of the bleeding. Immediately a nurse pushed two more milligrams of morphine though his IV line without asking. Another bandage was stuck to his testicles, both of which were lying outside of what was left of the scrotum.

Wonder where the other half of the scrotum is? Would have been helpful, I thought, but I did not say that aloud. He had managed to wipe the dirt out of one eye and was carefully watching me now as I surveyed all the damage. A bullet had entered the outside of his right thigh, passed under the femur and then blasted through the medial thigh and through his scrotum. This wound was different from most of the others I had seen—high velocity but no significant exit blast. This usually means armor piercing sniper rounds. My mental analysis would later be confirmed by his unit commander.

"Hey doc," the patient now with the dirt cleared from his eyes pulled me close to his head. "Can you save the boys? I have three kids, but if I live through this I might get married again and have some more."

"You are going home with all the boys," I said without commenting about his getting married again.

I then proceeded to notify the OR. One of the general surgeons came back with me. He decided he wanted to explore the femoral vessels.

"Even though his nerves and vessels appear to be intact?" I inquired.

"Mechanism of injury" he insisted, which meant that he wanted to open the soldier's leg to explore all of the vessels in case there was a major injury not obvious from the outside, despite the fact that the wounded man was neurologically intact, had a warm leg, and bounding pulses in his extremity. I didn't like his decision and decided I would talk to Lieutenant Colonel Bailey before going to the OR and let him know of my concerns.

On the way back I noticed that the reporter and cameraman from *USA Today* were following us. They had been with us all week and had been on the chopper that went out to pick up this patient. They were great guys, serious journalists, out to tell our story. Many reporters come here acting like tourists, but these two were very different. I liked and respected them.

In the OR, we prepped the infantryman's leg and the scrotum. He had good pulses in the leg, and it was completely intact neurologically. I hoped the general surgeon's exploration was for mechanism of injury and not just for the press. The "wanting to explore general surgeon" agreed that since his leg seemed fine I should proceed with my part of the case, and then he would follow.

Just after we prepped and draped the entire scrotum and leg, more choppers landed and another trauma call came in. The nurse came into the room and announced another gunshot wound to the head and shoulder.

"One of our guys," she added.

The general surgeon who was planning to explore the infantryman's leg stepped away from the table and took off his gown and gloves.

"The orthopedic surgeons will be in to look at these leg wounds and wash them out," he announced as he ran off to the ER to see if he could take charge of the newly arrived patients. The news reporter and photographer stayed put, wanting to see the outcome of the patient they had followed from the battlefield to the chopper and to here.

I proceeded to debride and reconstruct the testicles, and then replaced them back into the scrotum, or what was left of it. The scrotum just barely stretched enough to cover "his boys," but they were covered.

Orthopedic surgeons cleaned the leg wounds and irrigated them with nine liters of irrigation solution.

"What about the vessels?" I asked.

"They were intact in the ER, and he has great distal pulses in his feet. Why would anyone explore his vessels?" was the orthopedic surgeon's response.

The patient's wounds were dressed, and he was moved to the ICU for recovery.

Later as he woke from general anesthesia, the nurses reported that he started feeling for a necklace. Not just the dog tags, but a necklace.

"Hey where is my necklace? I got to have it," he repeated over and over again, searching around his neck. "Got to have it. Need to get it. Is it in the chopper? Got to have it. The necklace, I got to have it."

Patients in Iraq say a lot of things when they are first waking up from anesthesia. Things like "get down," "take cover," "IED ahead," "incoming," and when they wake up they stop. This patient, however, did not stop. He continued to ask for the necklace.

The nurses called the Patient Admission and Disposition (PAD) area in charge of weapons and personal belongings to inquire about the necklace. It was with his ring in the safe. They brought both of them, and he immediately put them on and fell asleep. Finally at peace, safe, comfortable, and reunited with objects of great importance to him.

I briefed his commander about the soldier's condition and the commander filled me in on the details. Sniper fire. Three hit. Two superficial. One serious: my patient.

"What happened to the sniper?" I asked.

"Well, we won't know for several days. The sniper's position, in a group of buildings, was pretty well destroyed. We pounded it with thousands of rounds and mortars, and finally, several 500-pound bombs—special delivery from the Air Force. We might never know."

Later when our patient was awake, his commander asked our commander for a Purple Heart medal to give to him before he left for Germany. His entire squad had now arrived with all of their weapons, and still wearing body armor. Their weapons stayed in the ready position, fingers positioned on the side just above the trigger. They had flown in for the award ceremony.

With almost all infantry units there is a sense of closeness that seems deeper than even family ties. I suppose that we rarely rely on our families for actual life and death situations, as our soldiers rely upon their battle buddies. They very literally rely on each other to do their jobs in life and death situations, not just once, but every time they patrol or go on a mission and every time they deploy, which for some units is often. The infantry units deploy for twelve to eighteen months during which they patrol for two days and have one day to rest and clean their gear. This was clearly one of those units, but there was a sense of something more here. Something else was holding them together and drawing them to this patient.

The captain awarded the Purple Heart, pinned to the pillow because he did not have a shirt, as the *USA Today* camera man shot pictures in rapid fire succession. Tears streaked down dirty faces of all his entire squad, battle buddies, one-and-all, and the rest of us who in a voyeuristic way looked in on the ceremony from a distance but were clearly not part of their unit.

We completed his paperwork to evacuate to Germany later the same night, hoping that he would continue on to Fort Carson in the next several days.

As his commander prepared to leave, one of the nurses walked him out to the parking lot. "He really wanted the necklace he came in with. He kept asking for it," she mentioned. "What was that all about?"

"Oh, that. His mother gave him the necklace when he was young. Three weeks before we deployed, his wife died in an accident. He has not taken it off since. He left his three kids with his parents and came here with his unit. He got the necklace back didn't he?" asked the captain.

I reflected back on his question, "Hey Doc, can you save the boys? I have three kids, but if I live through this I might get married again and have some more."

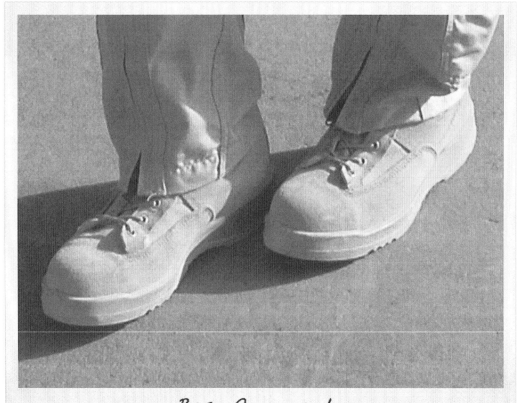

Base Commander

# Chapter 20

———

# COUNTERATTACK, COUNTERATTACK

3/10/06

During one of my many late nights as a surgical resident, I remember being exhausted after being up for about twenty-six hours and being in the OR treating a patient with a gunshot wound to the abdomen. As the junior resident, I was operating with the staff surgeon while the chief resident operated on another gunshot-wound patient in the next OR. The attending surgeon had been with us the entire twenty-six hours, and he was tired as well.

"If you do this enough when you're totally exhausted it will become part of you, and despite fatigue you will be on top of your game," he counseled me.

There is no question that repetition of any skill, even when you are totally toasted, will help you learn the task. This is certainly true with surgery.

Recently we have had an increase in mortar attacks, with mortars landing very close to the hospital. Last week at about 2300 hours, just as several hundred soldiers inside the Sustainer Movie Theater on Balad Air Base were leaving, a mortar exploded next to the theater. Several people were hit with rocks and debris, but there were no serious injuries. The hospital is only a few blocks from the theater.

I was in the hospital seeing patients when the first mortar landed, seconds later another one landed near the housing area, and then a third outside the wire. As the base "big voice" speaker screamed, "Incoming, incoming," the mortars landed and shook the walls of the tent. The mortars seemed to be much closer than they actually were. Nevertheless, the warning and explosions sent us diving under the tables and scrambling to the metal storage boxes outside the tents. When alarm red sounded, we rushed to get on our body armor and pile into the bunkers outside the hospital.

We had a house full of infantry patients on the ward when the mortars landed and the tents shook. As soon as the explosions sounded patients went from sound asleep and heavily medicated to wide awake searching under their beds yelling, "Where's my weapon? It's time to go to work. Hey, where is my weapon?"

This same scene played out simultaneously in the inpatient ward and in the self-care ward, housing about five patients. Soldier's weapons are locked in the cage at the Patient Admission Disposition center, not under the beds of men who are on narcotics for pain medication.

This week we admitted a Major Hamilton who had been trying to pass a three millimeter stone for several weeks without success. The stone had made its way down the ureter to his bladder but not out of the ureter, and his pain was becoming unbearable, so he urgently came to the clinic seeking help. He is the commander of an intelligence unit responsible for base security. His office monitors incoming mortar attacks, patrols the area around the base, and is responsible for counterattacks against mortars. Every time the base gets mortared, his office tracks the incoming mortar, sends the big voice warning signal, and then returns fire with a barrage of three or more mortars to the area where the incoming mortar originated, just to recognize their attack effort and warn them that we will not sit still while they try to kill us! Finally, he sends troops to the area where the mortar originated to destroy the sender, if he can be found, and destroy any additional mortars in the area. He may even call in a Predator aircraft for special package delivery or an F-16 if one is in the area.

Now, however, he was being attacked from an enemy inside, one he had never seen. We admitted him, gave him pain medication, but after several days he was unable to pass the stone, so we took him to the OR and passed a small basket to dislodge the stone from his ureter. He was slow to wake up from anesthesia. While he was just coming out of anesthesia and had started breathing on his own, we moved him to the recovery room.

At about 0830 hours he was wheeled into recovery just as a mortar exploded several blocks from the hospital in the H-6 housing area. Immediately after the first mortar, a second landed near the same area. As the second mortar exploded, the major sat straight up on the cot and, despite still being under the influence of anesthesia, yelled "Counterattack! Counterattack! Find their sector. Send mortars now. Lets move it! Counterattack! Counterattack! Wait, where am I?"

"In the hospital. Look you even have a catheter," his nurse said pointing to the red tube coming out from his penis.

"Oh, this is not good. I need a counterattack," he said.

Then he laid down and was instantly asleep.

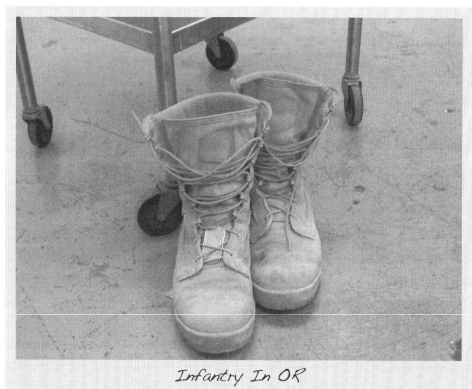

Infantry In OR

# Chapter 21

———

# I THINK HE IS ONE OF YOUR PATIENTS

3/9/06

Sergeant Ponly was a twenty-five-year-old soldier who came into my clinic with classic prostate and bladder problems, some burning when he urinated, a weak stream, and frequent urination. This was not new; he had endured these symptoms for years, but now he was putting his platoon in jeopardy because he had to stop frequently to urinate while out on patrol. Patrols are frequently shot at while stopped. Ponly was in charge of a platoon of about twenty men who were assigned to patrol the streets as infantry soldiers.

When he presented to the clinic he was in full battle armor and held his M-4 in the ready position on the other side of my desk while I took his history. His M-4 was fully equipped with night vision illumination, laser scope, Luminex digital finger activated flashlight, and grenade or .203 launcher. I gave him permission to set his firearm down but he seemed reluctant.

"We almost never take small-arms fire here. I have been here for the past month and have not had to return any small arms fire, but you can keep your gear right there on the floor, just in case."

I gave him permission to remove it all: his helmet with night-vision goggle clip, sand goggles, body armor with neck, shoulder, groin attachments, seven M-16 ammo clips, shot gun rounds, four grenades, and three .203 rounds. One of the .203 round holders was empty.

"Hey you missed one," I said pointing to the empty hole on the end of .203 rounds storage area.

"Nope, used it just before I jumped the chopper to come here," he said without even looking down.

I believed him.

"Where did you come from?"

"Hawija," he replied.

"Show me on the map behind you," I said, pointing to the four-by-four-foot map of Iraq one of the intelligence officers had printed for me several weeks earlier.

"Right here," he said, pointing to a small town not far from Kirkuk.

I circled it with a red magic marker. Infantry soldiers who come to us loaded with weapons and still wearing their armor are always from extremely dangerous places like Hawija. In war you learn that first and foremost, you have to protect yourself. As a physician about to examine the sergeant's private parts, I was certain I would be safer if he was separated from his weapons, even if only by ten feet.

After a careful history and examination, I decided what he really needed was a cystoscopy, in which I insert a catheter sized telescope scope inside the urethra, down into the penis and all the way into the bladder to look for a stricture or narrowing of the urethra, which would cause his symptoms.

He reluctantly agreed, and I moved him another ten feet farther from his gear to the cysto table to perform the procedure. He did not have a stricture, but instead had an unusual finding of a type of urethral valves that blocked his urine from getting out. Essentially, it amounted to a one-way valve positioned the wrong way. His bladder showed deep trabeculations, common for a seventy-year-old man, but not a twenty-five year old. I admitted him and scheduled his surgical procedure the following day.

Unfortunately, we did not have all of the equipment for valve ablation. What I really needed was something like a crochet hook, but small enough to pass alongside the scope so I could hook it and either tear it away or lift it up and ablate it with the laser. I immediately remembered one of the older sisters from our service members group at church was constantly crocheting with small hooks. I called her. She brought a metal crochet hook, which I sterilized and then used for the procedure. I performed a simple ablation of the valves and left a bladder catheter in for about a week.

I sterilized the knitting hook again and then tried to return it. She did not seem to want to touch it, and recommended I keep it in case I need it again later.

"A gift for the war effort," she suggested.

Sergeant Ponly did what most of the infantry and cavalry soldiers do when admitted. He slept and ate. Soldiers arrive physically exhausted and often emotionally worn. To be in a relatively safe place with angelic nurses and technicians seeing to their needs and comfort is such a relief that they sleep for days. They sink into the cots, cover their heads, occasionally put in some ear plugs and fade off into a deep sleep most have not had since they arrived in Iraq for a twelve-month tour of duty.

The 332nd is a place where people come to live. There is peace here and it feels safe—a luxury many at forward operating bases do not enjoy. So here they sleep, not for hours, but days. And Sergeant Ponly was no different. Like most soldiers admitted to the self-care ward, he slept fourteen to twenty hours a day for about six days, waking only to eat. Having a catheter in the penis for several days while the urethra heals and the bladder rests also has a way of discouraging activity.

He emailed the troops in his unit to update them daily. The men he leads are barely adults, but they are old in wisdom and aged with the experience of war. They had come to rely on his experience and leadership and were reluctant to go out on patrol without him, their platoon leader. Thus they wanted daily updates on his progress and the expected date of his return to Hawija. Finally on day six, I pulled his catheter and redid the cystocopy to make sure he did not have any significant healing left to do. The urethra looked great and wide open. I filled his bladder and sent him outside to use the portable toilets in the parking lot.

"Great stream, Doc. I have never pissed like that. When can I go back to work? The boys need me!"

He spent the rest of the day at the Base Exchange and moving around base. Well rested, pockets full of snacks from the closet for his boys, and with new found satisfaction from the simple pleasure of fantastic urinary flow, he caught a chopper to Hawija to go back on patrol with his platoon.

About two weeks later I was passing through the ER when one of the doctors told me an old patient was back to see me, and wanted me to know he still had a great, strong stream.

"Where is he," I asked.

"In the CT scanner. He and these three here in the ER got jacked up when an RPG sniper shot their Hummer with a grenade and set them all on fire. Well, not all on fire, just the top of the Hummer and their heads. Your patient has a bad burn to his face and a busted nose. Just dropped him off in radiology for films. You should go see him. He seemed anxious to talk to you."

A soldier was in the scanner, but with his swollen face, brightly burned nose, peeling skin, and all the blood, I did not recognize him at first. He recognized me.

"Hey Doc what's up," he said. I recognized the voice, but that was all. When he saw the puzzled look on my face, he cheerfully said, "Oh, no, I must be bad off. You don't recognize me. I am Sergeant Ponly."

"Ponly, what happened to you guys?"

"Well, remember that place you circled on your map in red? I told you it was a dangerous place to be."

He then retold the story of being on patrol. Somewhere from the side a sniper shot the Humvee with an RPG. Smoke filled the cabin, and the fire from the fuel cell in the back sucked out the air. The driver jumped out of the truck to put out the fire on his head and vest. The truck proceeded to move forward crashing into two cars, blocking Ponly's door on the front right and Brigg's door, on the back right. They pushed on the doors, but they would not open. Small arms fire rang out all around them, hitting the Hummer and the trucks in their platoon. The front truck with the .50 caliber machine gun turned all the way around and came back to lay down fire. Others jumped out from the safe haven of their trucks to return fire and to pull the others from the burning vehicle. Ponly had a serious nose fracture with a large hematoma in his nose and sinus, and a first-degree burn on his nose and face. The others were all burned on the face, hands, and chest. They would be evacuated to Germany.

Sergeant Ponly went to the OR for Dr. Powers to reduce his open fracture and reconstruct his nose. Despite his serious and painful injuries, he never showed any signs of pain or emotion until he asked me how the others were, and then told me how frustrated he had been with his door jammed up against another car and not being able to get out to help Briggs, who was sitting behind him with his helmet and vest on fire.

Only the thought of his squad being injured caused this soldier any real pain. Big tears welled up in his face.

"I really hate to see any of my boys hurt, Doc," he said while the tears filled his eyes and ran down his cheeks.

Now you must be reminded that Sergeant Ponly is only twenty-five, and the members of his squad are eighteen and nineteen years old. But they are his boys, and when they hurt, he hurts. Once again I am reminded of the unique bond formed in war when lives are saved by the courage, bravery, and selfless actions of others. Leaders care for their unit members, and the boys lay down lives for the leaders, who would do the same for them. That's why the .50 caliber gunner continues to fire at the enemy even when he is getting fired on from the front and back, leaving large holes and dents on both sides of his turret. None of these guys stop and ask, "Am I going to die for the guy next to me?" Instead they act and react to protect each other without much thought as to the consequences, and too often those consequences include death.

Later I would joke with Sergeant Ponly about his being lucky enough to know he is wearing the Purple Heart. He apologetically tells me about the Bronze Star his commander submitted for him because of his courageous actions in a wildfire fight in November.

I pushed for more details, and he told the story. His platoon had been pinned down by a large insurgent group in an ambush from three directions. He moved his trucks into a circle to return fire. He then gathered the wounded from a truck that had been hit in the first wave of the attack; all the while he was engaging the enemy and calling in air support that finally subdued the enemy attackers. Several of his boys were wounded, but he was able to return them all alive. He reminded me that others in his platoon had already been rewarded the Bronze Star, but only the recipient's loved ones knew about it. In the Army the Bronze Star is most often given to someone who dies in a heroic action.

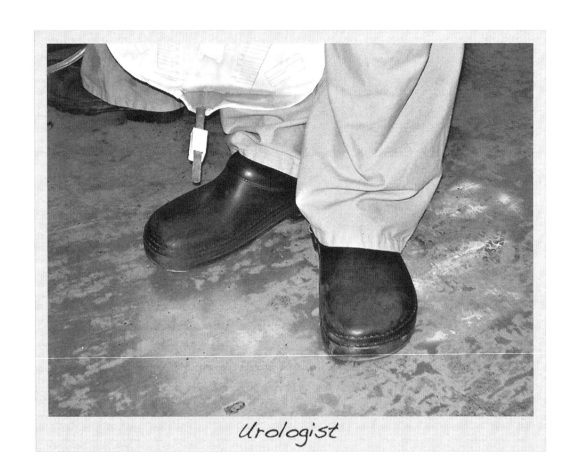

*Urologist*

# Chapter 22

---

# REGULAR DAY

3/13/06
Six patients injured from IED attacks, and four gunshot wounds admitted today. Operated all day and evening: bladders, kidneys, testis, and scrotum. I am exhausted. Going to bed early. Can't write any more today.

Reservist

## Chapter 23

———

# DISCOVERY BY CAMEL

3/14/06

This morning we had a trauma call for several soldiers injured when their convoy, traveling from Kuwait to Baghdad struck a herd of camels. Convoys get close together, drive at near maximum speed, about sixty to seventy miles per hour, and try not to stop for anything. Stopping along the route puts the entire convoy at risk for being attacked by IED, RPG, mortars, or small-arms fire. No one wants to stop. Rolling fast decreases the chance that several vehicles will be damaged in the face of an IED roadside attack.

While this convoy was rolling towards Baghdad loaded with supplies, a herd of camels ran out into the road. One of the drivers of a large tractor trailer rig, an up-armored eighteen-wheeler, swerved to miss one camel, but when the rest of the herd ran in front of him, he swerved back and ran right into the camel he had been trying to avoid. There was a loud thud and then a big crash as the camel smashed into the rig. The driver bounced up and hit his head on the roof of the cab, knocking him unconscious momentarily. He and several others injured in the camel incident were flown to the 332nd.

His head and neck were secured in a C collar, and he was sent off to the CT scanner. In addition, a full-body scan was done to search for any internal injuries. The radiologist called to tell me that he had significant dilation of both kidneys, called hydronephrosis, as well as a left sided ureteral stent.

I quickly went to the ER to see if his chemistry studies had returned from the panel of blood samples that are routinely sent on all trauma patients. His kidneys were so dilated that it looked like he did not have any remaining kidney function. His basic metabolic panel confirmed my fears. The serum creatinine, or gauge of his kidney function, should have been 1.0 but was 3.3, well within the renal failure range. I cancelled the Toradol (nonsteroidal anti-inflammatory drug) order from the ER, which had it been administered might have completely sent him into renal failure. On further questioning about his medical history, he suddenly remembered that he was treated for a kidney stone just three months before coming to Iraq; the urologist had left a stent in.

I took him to the OR and removed the heavily calcified stent and placed a bladder catheter, then repeated the CT scan the following day. His kidneys had completely decompressed. He had unrecognized, or at least ignored, vesicoureteral reflux (bad valves in the bladder allowing urine to reflux into the kidneys) and renal insufficiency bordering on renal failure. He was not going back to his unit to run convoys. He was going to Germany, then Walter Reed, and then home. He needed a very complex work-up and possibly surgery to fix his ureters, if it was not too late to save any reasonable kidney function. He pleaded to go back to his unit. They were already short ten men due to death and injury. Now he would be number eleven. He cried.

I signed the papers and sent him to Germany.

Marine Corps Infantry

# Chapter 24

---

# MORTARED AGAIN

3/15/06

Recent rains had toppled some of the sand bags in one of the housing areas, so we went to help fill up new bags and to restack them to fortify the trailers to about six feet from the ground. Just as the sun was setting we heard sirens and then the alarm. We went straight to the ground. The C-RAM (counter rocket, artillery, mortar), which spits out several waves of rapid fire spray of machine gun bullets, went off hitting one of the incoming mortars creating an impressive explosion that sent fragments tumbling into the parking lot of the hospital. We were very excited to hear that it was the first successful hit from the C-RAM.

The Balad Air Base has several C-RAM systems strategically located around the base because of the frequency of mortar attacks at the base. The C-RAM is also known to the Navy as the PHALANX and provides U.S. Navy ships with a "last-chance" defense against anti-ship missiles and littoral warfare threats that have penetrated other fleet defenses. It automatically detects, tracks and engages anti-air warfare threats such as anti-ship missiles, aircraft and, at Balad, mortars and rockets. Each system must successfully identify, track, and engage the incoming threat munitions.

The system must also demonstrate a capability to destroy the threat while minimizing collateral damage, which is no small task given the proximity of Balad City and the constant incoming and outgoing airplanes and helicopters.

Later in the week Major Hamilton came to have his stent removed. He told me the rest of the story. With not a little excitement, he told me that intelligence had anticipated a mortar attack that day and correctly expected it in the sector where it originated. Two F-16s were circling in the area of the anticipated origin, and a Predator was also in the area for observation. As soon as the mortar was launched, it was tracked back to its origin, where two trucks were observed pulling away. While the C-RAM destroyed the mortar over the hospital tents, the F-16s and Predator tracked the two fleeing vehicles. Several platoons scrambled to follow the trucks to their destination. Shortly after they reached their homes, the platoons arrived, kicked in the doors, arrested four men, and confiscated eight IEDs, six mortar tubes, and two caches of weapons and mortars. Great teamwork on the part of the entire system.

*Pharmacist*

# Chapter 25

———

# MORTARS ON C COMPANY

3/15/06

Fourteen soldiers from C Company 2$^{nd}$ of the 502$^{nd}$ were admitted all at once in one big mass-casualty situation after being hit with a mortar. Most suffered superficial wounds, but all had multiple injuries. The 10$^{th}$ combat support hospital at Baghdad took the most seriously injured patients; about six total, and sent the rest to us. Of the patients who came to Balad, five of them were put in the ENT and urology clinic to watch TV and wait to have their wounds washed and dressed. There was only one seriously injured. At first he seemed to only have a small full-thickness laceration wound on the forehead, just above the eye, but when he started to have neurological changes in the ER he was moved up to "immediate" status and sent directly to the CT scanner.

In the regular x-ray room there was another member of the C Company who continued to ask everyone who would listen about the status of his battle buddy, the one with a small wound over his eye and changing mental status. He was repeatedly assured that his buddy was doing well, but actually his condition continued to worsen. The head CT scan showed that a small metal fragment had passed into the skull above the eye and traversed the brain on one side, finally coming to rest far from the entrance site in the back of his head. He continued to deteriorate and was quickly moved to the OR for an exploration of his brain and craniectomy, in which the skull is removed from one side to allow the brain to swell under the protection of the skin, but safe from damage that would result from swelling within the confines of the bony intact skull.

His battle buddy's inquiries escalated to a near panic as he demanded to know the status of his friend. He repeatedly asked if they would both be going to Germany together.

Finally he cried out, "Please, please, please you can't let him die. Don't let him die. He is my lifelong best friend. We grew up together. He is going to marry my sister in June when we return. Please don't let him die."

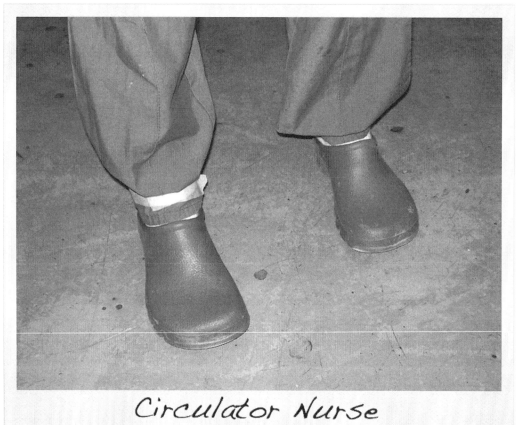

Circulator Nurse

## Chapter 26

---

# EVAPORATING HAND CLEANER CAN GET YOU THE WORLD

3/19/06

I recently cared for a Navy Seal who introduced himself as Joe Smith. About thirty minutes and five milligrams of morphine later, he leaned over, grabbed my arm and whispered, "Hey Doc, what name did I give you?"

"Excuse me? Are you talking to me Joe Smith?" I replied.

"Oh, yeah, Smith. That's me, Smith," he laughed.

I admitted him for kidney stones and treated both his right and left sides. He had ureteral stents in for awhile and after fourteen days was ready to leave. He came to my office to thank me for the care but suddenly wanted to tell some stories. He and his squad had been protecting the Syrian border, where they found an average of six hundred pounds of explosives a day, all poorly hidden in trucks, cars, and trailers.

"What is the wildest thing you have seen?" I asked him, and then listened intently.

They were out on patrol one afternoon and a young man approached them. They immediately assumed he was a suicide bomber, fired a warning shot signaling him to stop, and then had him show that he was not wired. He informed them that he knew where some men were making IEDs in his neighborhood. "Smith" and his squad immediately offered him cash to show them the house, but he did not want cash. Instead he wanted hand cleaner gel, lots of it. They had a case in a truck so they gave him half of it.

"Why hand gel?" someone asked.

"I love the smell, the clean feeling of my hands, and like magic it tingles and then disappears."

In their plain, non-military, pickup trucks, they followed the young man with incredibly clean hands as he repeatedly used the gel from a bottle in his pocket, spraying, smelling, and rubbing over and over again along the route. The boy stopped in front of an unassuming home, and then actually walked onto a porch and pointed to the house.

"This is the house," he said in Arabic. He then took his half case of hand gel and turned toward home.

Because the boy acted so comfortable on the porch, their suspicion of a trap was high. They tried the front door, which was locked and did not seem to be wired. Two blasts from one of their shotguns opened the locks. The squad stormed in to find an insurgent at the kitchen table soldering wires for an IED activation device. Two other men came from different rooms in the house to see what had caused all of the commotion, and then a few minutes later two more pulled up and parked in the front. They entered all surprised to see six white men with long hair and beards pointing AK 47 rifles at them.

All in all the squad found five stolen cars (one already wired with a trunk full of explosives), two Russian sniper rifles, RPGs, many large mortar shells for making IEDS, lots of grenades, suicide vests, and several AK-47 rifles.

Hand gel—good for lots of uses and can even make insurgents disappear.

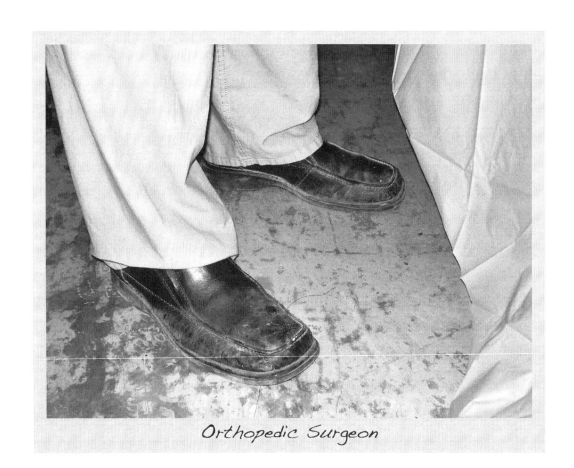

Orthopedic Surgeon

# Chapter 27

---

# USING UROLOGY LASER TO HELP ORTHOPEDIC SURGERY

3/19/06

This has been a busy weekend. Sunday morning we took in six patients—all Special Forces. Two had been killed in action before arrival, and four had been wounded with large ball bearings, shrapnel from a suicide bomb. During an early morning raid of a suspected insurgent's home, the suspect detonated himself just after the squad entered. It was obviously a setup to kill the Special Forces squad, and it nearly did.

One of the squad had a large ball bearing embedded in the knee just below the joint. The orthopedic surgeon on call had been trying to dislodge it without making a large incision in his knee. I had been waiting for several hours to get a stone patient to the OR and would occasionally wander near the room and look inside to see if they were making progress. I had evaluated the films from radiology and suddenly realized that the ball bearing appeared to be the size of my flexible cystoscope. I offered a different plan from using the hemostat, or worse, opening the tendon and soft tissue wider to grasp it under direct vision. Instead, we used the flexible cystoscope, which was a perfect match for the tract the bearing had created. Once we could see the ball bearing, I used the holmium laser to chip away one millimeter of the bone, freeing the bearing from the grip of the bone, and then entrapped it with a stone basket and extracted it through the same tract. This procedure caused no more damage than the projectile itself had created.

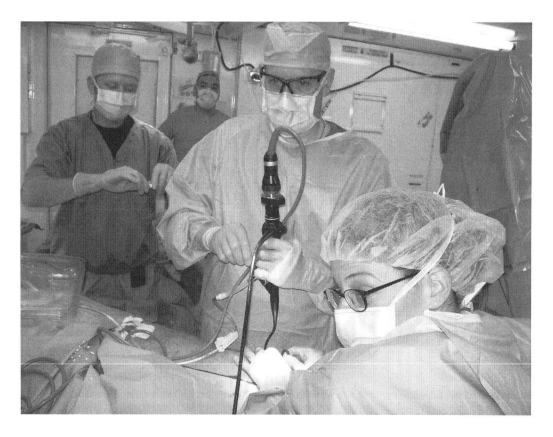

Figure 13. Instead of making a large incision, a flexible cystoscope is inserted into the hole created above the knee joint by one of many ball bearings taped to the suicide bomber.

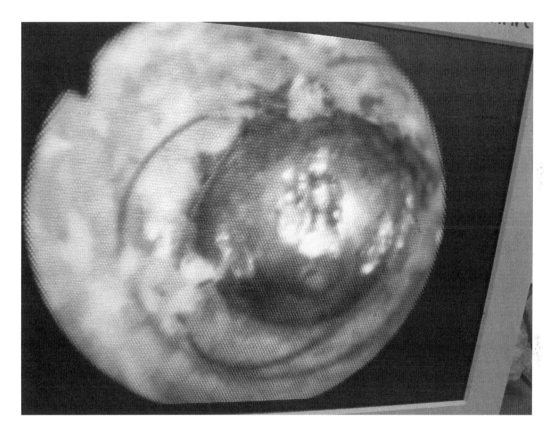

Figure 14. The ball bearing fragment is freed from surrounding bone with a kidney stone laser and then extracted using a kidney stone wire basket.

Platoon Sergeant

# Chapter 28

————

# THE LUCKIEST MAN IN THE HOSPITAL TODAY

3/20/06

One of the exciting aspects of emergency medicine is not knowing what will come through the doors next. This morning a squad was hit with an IED while riding in their up-armored Humvees. Three were admitted with fragment wounds to the legs and arms. The platoon leader was riding front right when the bomb struck the door. He had a deep laceration on his right upper hip and back and was covered from head to toe with fine dust or sand from the explosion. He was sitting in an up-right position on the NATO cot while Sergeant Stack was trying to remove his body armor. Sergeant Stack was only about five feet tall and the Marine platoon leader was about six foot four. His body armor included six grenades, seven ammo clips, a flashlight, radio, and head set. Sergeant Stack had the bottom of the vest balanced on her head trying to hold it up while she tugged and pulled, questioning why the vest would not pull away from the right side of his back. Each time she pulled the Marine winced.

He finally said, "Ma'am, I think I may have broken a rib or two because every time you tug on my vest it sends a sharp pain into my side."

I watched all of this unfold as I walked through the ER on the way to the OR. The techs were busy caring for the others and clearly the nurse needed some helping hands to get the vest off. I grasped the shoulder of the vest with my left hand and immediately realized that it weighted about one hundred pounds. I used both hands to stabilize it while Sergeant Stack worked to free it from his back. She produced trauma scissors from seemingly nowhere and quickly started cutting away the inside of the vest, which was mysteriously welded to the soldier's skin. The scissors hit solid metal. She glanced at a dent in the blades of the scissors, backed off a few inches and continued trimming until the vest was free. With some effort I lowered the freed vest to the ground as Sergeant Stack nudged me with her shoulder.

"Wow! You should see this!" she said.

I looked up to see a ten-by-two-and-a-half-inch chunk of metal that had hit the hip, taken a matching size piece of skin and muscle from the side, and then pierced the vest bouncing off the inside of his armor, entering the skin, bouncing off a rib, exiting the skin, and entering the vest again. In addition, the heat of the metal had created a third-degree burn.

Once the vest was cut away, we could see that the piece of metal was stuck to his back by a thin three-by-two-inch skin bridge, seared white and devitalized by the recently red-hot fragment. Crowds soon formed and the Marine, anxious to see the trophy carefully secured under his skin, asked to see for himself. A digital photo revealed to him the situation,

"Incredible. This is going on my mantel at home!"

The skin bridge was cut away and the fragment removed and handed to the Marine.

"That was close," he remarked.

He looked down at his right hip and tenderly touched the full thickness burn.

"Looks pretty good. I need to get going back the unit."

"Not so fast," the plastic surgeon countered.

To him it looked like a deep flesh wound, to the rest of us it looked like the injury was deep and serious. It would take a trip to the OR for debridement of burned, devitalized tissue, and then a transfer to the States, for skin grafting. With big tears in his eyes, not because of the pain from his injury, the sergeant begged not to be sent home. We listened once again to the appeals of a leader needing to stay with his unit, needing to lead his men, needing to care for the boys for whom he was responsible.

The patient with his large metal souvenir was dispatched to Germany, and then to Walter Reed for further care.

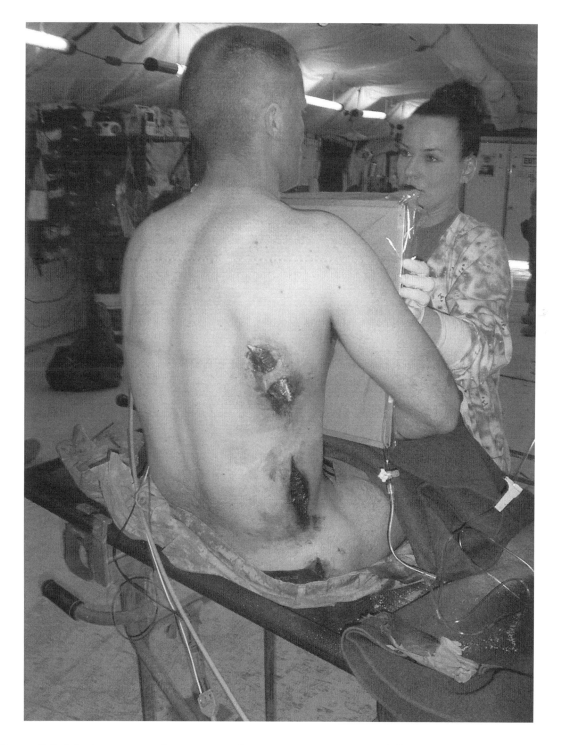

Figure 15. Marine gets a chest x-ray after an IED sent a metal fragment bouncing off his hip and ribs finally coming to rest under his skin.

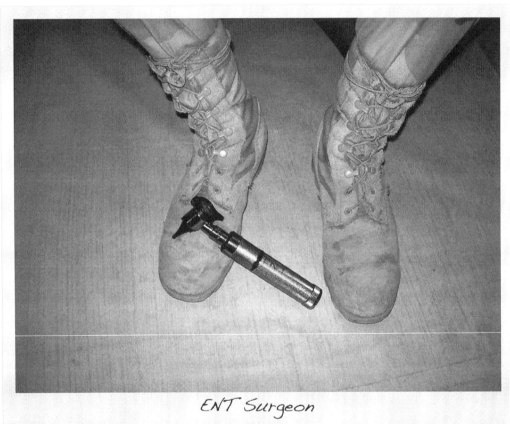

ENT Surgeon

# Chapter 29

———

# COORDINATED ATTACK

3/22/06

The urology clinic was located in the same tent as the ENT clinic. Regularly the ENT surgeon examines patients recently exposed to IEDs. I can tell when they are in the clinic because he has to raise his voice for them to hear over the ringing in their ears and the broken ear drums. This was the case today. To get out of my clinic, I have to go through the ENT clinic. A call came from the ER. I opened the door to the ENT clinic to see nine Marines, all sitting in the ENT office.

The Marines at the forward bases often have the hardest and most dangerous jobs in the war. When they need housing in strategic areas, they knock on doors and persuade the Iraqis to rent them their homes. This is what one platoon of Marines had done in a small village outside the city of Ramadi. The three-story home they rented was big enough for all nine of them. It was in a good location on a major road and had been used to help control the small village, a refuge for insurgents. The Marines established a small well-positioned compound by taking several homes, setting up wire barriers around the city block and stacking sand bags to the top of the lower level windows. On a regular basis their position had taken and withstood mortar attacks. When mortared, several Marines would go to the roof top to see if they could determine the origin of the "stick" and act as a lookout from the secured position.

Late last night the mortars started raining down, one after another in a sustained attack. Several Marines went to the rooftop to determine the location. They identified the origin of the mortars, returned fire, and called in a ground strike. As the ground strike convoy moved down the main road toward the mortar fire, roadside IEDs began to explode. There were nine total. Only four detonated, but enough to shut down the traffic in both directions leading to and from the village. As soon as the IEDs went off, a large petroleum truck crashed through the Marine barriers. Guards fired on the driver. The suicide driver managed to get the fuel truck in front of one home just as he detonated the explosives. Because of the sand bags, barriers and armored trucks on the side of the road the structural damage from the blast was limited to blown-out windows.

Human damage was more serious. Nine Marines suffered broken eardrums, but luckily there were few serious injuries and no fatalities. All nine were taken to the ENT office, where they sat for several hours. One by one they were carefully examined and then returned to duty.

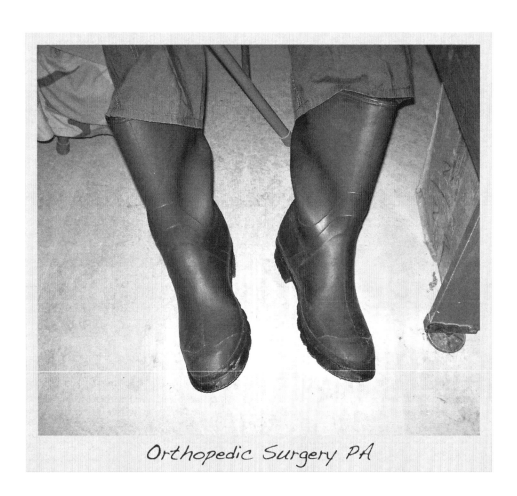

Orthopedic Surgery PA

# Chapter 30

———

# DON'T TAKE THE FARMERS' WATER

3/22/06

Water is a prerequisite for life in general and a source of constant conflict worldwide. There is a large strong stream from the Euphrates River that feeds many sustenance farms around our base. Because insurgents had been using the water to get close to the base, U.S. forces countered by diverting the water away from the area.

As a result local farmers, who usually do not support the insurgents, have now joined forces in the mortar effort. This is due, in part, to their frustration over the diverted water and in part because the insurgents pay them for their assistance. My sources have told me that everyone in the Balad City area is one person away from someone with insurgent money. All you have to do is talk to one or two people, and you will be armed and financed for your efforts to kill U.S. forces.

The result is that we have been taking on a lot of mortar fire. This week in the early morning hours the sirens sounded and then came the big voice with the warning "In coming." I piled out of bed and hit the floor, covering my ears and eyes. The explosions were blocks away, but five mortars landed near the post office and gas station. We sustained no serious injuries, but it is only a matter of time. Eventually we'll take a direct hit. It seems the insurgents have no shortage of mortars and people willing to use them.

After recognizing the mistake in diverting the farmers' water, the river flow was restored, and within a week the mortar fire slowed to three times a day.

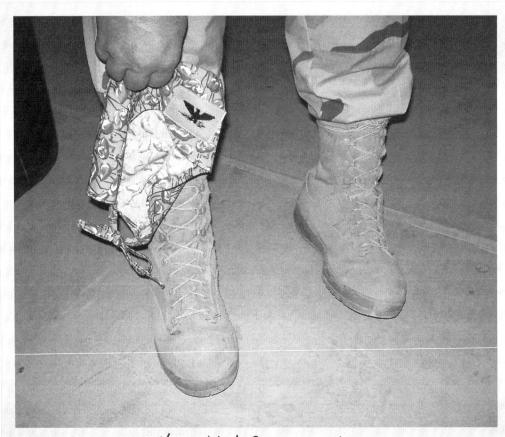

Hospital Commander

---

# Chapter 31

# THE INALIENABLE RIGHTS OF THE TESTIS: LIFE LIBERTY & THE PURSUIT OF HAPPINESS

3/24/06

The Marines have an unusual game in which they try to smack each other in the scrotum before the other can block the blow. Occasionally injuries occur. To date, I have taken out two dead testicles after traumatic rupture and delayed treatment resulting in ischemia, all due to the Marines' game. Last night we had a Marine who presented with an acute scrotum after he had been "smacked" earlier in the day. I took him to the OR and was able to fix the testis and stop the hemorrhaging from several large spermatic veins that had been torn and were actively bleeding.

Each morning all the command section players, surgeons, ER docs, ICU and nurse teams discuss the patients from the previous day's admission and briefly describe their injuries, treatment, and disposition. The slide for Corporal Lothamer said "acute scrotum," which prompted a question from the commander.

"Bishoff, what is an acute scrotum?"

This was a perfect opportunity to explain to the commander and the group the inalienable rights of the testicle, which are life, liberty and the pursuit of happiness. An acute scrotum is any condition which threatens these rights of the testicles.

By definition: *Life*—anything that puts the blood supply to the testis in jeopardy. Testicular torsion is an example. *Liberty*—the ability to move freely around the scrotum. Hydrocele, hernia, epididymitis, and infection can all cause restriction in movement, as can traumatic rupture. *Pursuit of happiness*—to find ova anywhere.

The commander turned around in his chair to look me directly in the eyes as most of the room laughed. With the straightest face I could muster I replied, "Yes sir. The inalienable rights of the testis."

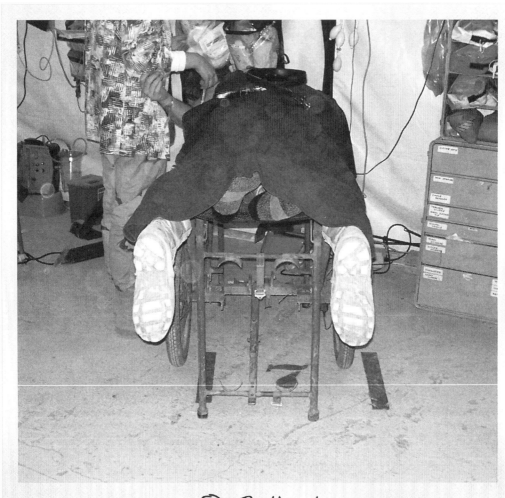

ED Patient

# Chapter 32

———

# OH, THAT STILL SMALL VOICE

3/26/06

Call it what you want: intuition, a hunch, a feeling, or the still small voice, but all of us, from time to time, have experienced strong impressions and may have regrets or good memories depending upon our diligence and action. Last night I went to bed rather late. I read scripture for about thirty minutes and then knelt to pray. Suddenly, I had the distinct impression that I should get on the floor and take cover. The impression was so strong that I grabbed some ear plugs and laid down. My heart was pounding. I covered my ears and eyes and waited. I was uncomfortable, but the impression was so strong I was convinced a mortar would land at anytime. After thirty minutes and no attack, I pulled out my sleeping bag and crawled inside, where I spent a restless night on the floor of the trailer. My impression was so intense that I could not easily fall asleep waiting for the explosion. It never came.

I spent today, Sunday, in the OR before going to church. Now this evening, after church and calling home, I am very tired. However, I do not regret obeying the prompting and impression I had received the previous night. Following the still small voice has served me well in the past, and as long as God wants me here on earth I am sure listening to that voice will continue to bless my life. The next time I have those feelings, I will be on the ground again.

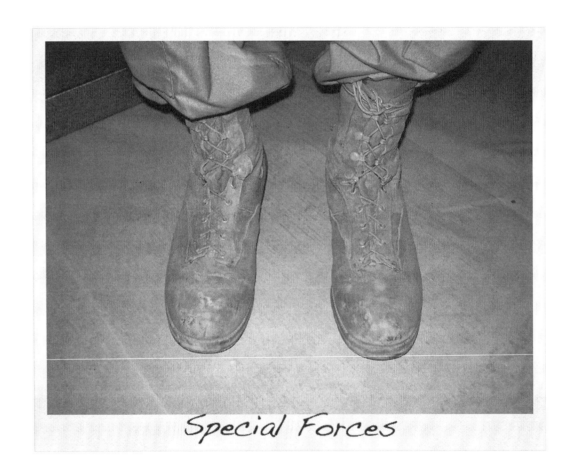

Special Forces

———

# Chapter 33

# SMASH CRASH GOOD MORNING

3/27/06

This afternoon, I was called to the ER and met a physician assigned to the Special Forces unit on base. He told me he had a patient who needed to be evaluated with ultrasound for a possible rupture of the testis, but he did not want the patient paraded through the hospital. Instead, he pulled a plain unmarked van around the back of the hospital to the CT scanner entrance. Three armed soldiers without any markings on their uniforms escorted a man about thirty years old wearing an orange jumpsuit into radiology. He had on goggles that had painted lenses to prevent sight, bandages on his bare feet, and metal handcuffs clamped tightly around his wrists.

A quick ultrasound showed his testis to have a large hematoma. He needed to have his testis explored and possibly removed. In the meantime he was taken to the ER and placed in a secure private room in the back to await his surgery.

Once the patient was anesthetized, I carefully examined his scrotum. He had a soft left testis consistent with rupture and a normal-feeling right testis. Exploration of this man's "acute scrotum" showed that all of the inalienable rights owed to the left testis were in jeopardy. There was not one, but two, holes in the testis with tubules extruding everywhere. Basically the testis had been shattered sorely affecting its pursuit of happiness and liberty. In addition, the removal of a large hematoma showed a thrombosed vein, which threatened the life of the testis. I debrided the nonviable tubules back to the normal testis, leaving about half intact. I closed the tunica, reconstructed the testis, evacuated the hematoma, and removed the thrombosed vein.

My efforts to get the whole story of this mysterious patient were gently rebuffed, so I stealthily resorted to my own intel gathering. I had discovered weeks earlier that we kept a "prison" of sorts for interrogating prisoners here at the Special Forces compound on Anaconda. Most of these special prisoners are sent to us from Abu Ghraib, but a few are actually from our own back yard.

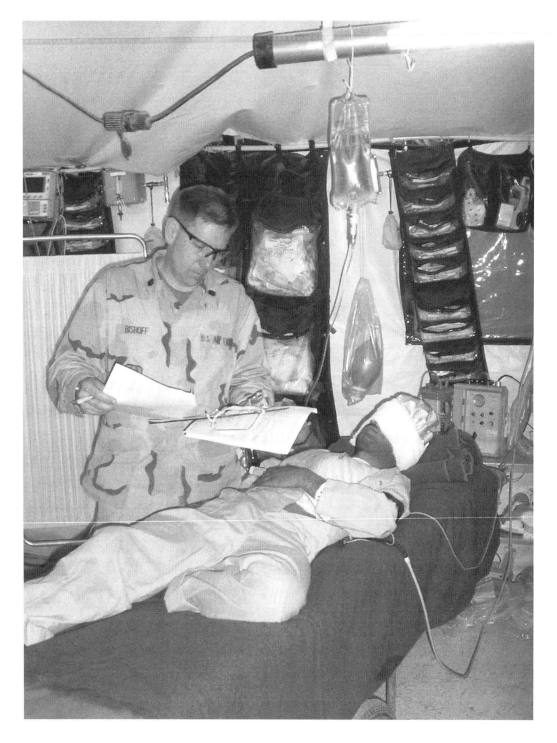

Figure 16. Insurgent patient brought to the 332nd for treatment of injuries.

After the surgery the guards were starting to trust me. Individually they added little to the total story, but in bits and pieces it was coming clear. The flight surgeon, an ER doc is his real life, added some interesting information. Apparently, there had been an early morning raid, a wake-up call to several insurgents, including this gentleman (patient number 1025) in his own home. On ropes attached to a hovering Black Hawk helicopter, Special Forces swung down and crashed in through his windows. Apparently they had been instructed to take him alive; otherwise he certainly would not have needed to be in the OR. With all the windows smashed and glass shards scattered all over the floor—no problem for shoes and boots, but a real problem for the bare footed suspect rudely awakened from sleep—Patient 1025 resisted enough to get his nose broken, lip split and to take a knee to the testis, which was proved significant enough.

The guards were quick to point out that he spoke English well, and that was why they were not willing to share any information with me about their home base.

One of the night guards asked if the military would fix his own deviated nose. I indicated that they would be happy to and then innocently asked the guard where he was going when he went home. He paused and then looked concerned. After several seconds he whispered, "I would prefer not to say out loud. I don't want this one to hear anything about us. Nothing at all."

"Well, I see," I responded. "When you get home go see the ENT docs and ask them. They will fix your nose for you."

When I told them that 1025 should be ready to leave in the morning, they seemed relieved. The guard with the deviated septum looked around the organized chaos that was our hospital and said, "That will be a great relief sir."

Guarding the patient in the back of ICU-1 with rolling curtain-like partitions as the only divider from the rest of the very busy ICU made them quite uneasy. It has been interesting to see how uncomfortable the Special forces that are guarding high level detainees become in the hospital. Our seemingly lax security made them very edgy. The free flow of Iraqi interpreters, third country nationals, and hospital personnel is not the strictly controlled environment they are used to. While in the hospital environment they gave up some of the control of their surroundings, and they were anxious to have control back on their side. The hospital also reminds them of the realities of war, and the reality here is not good.

F-16 Egress

# Chapter 34

――――

# YOU NEVER ASKED

3/27/06

At the gym I spotted one of the members of our LDS service-members church group. He always comes for church services but then leaves before they are over. I was just leaving and had a strong impression to go and say hello to him. He seemed pleasantly surprised at my approach, and I asked him about his day, which apparently had gone well.

"I can't remember where you work," I said.

"That is because you have never asked me," he responded.

And he was right I had not asked. I had assumed he was with the F-16 squadron from Hill AFB, Utah, but he was from Logan, Utah. He had joined the Air Force to get money for college and had not decided what to do with his life. His time in the Air Force had helped him grow up, mature, and start thinking about careers, including careers in medicine.

"Isn't that interesting," I said, "I have a career in medicine and would love to have you come to the hospital and visit."

He seemed interested. I made an appointment with him and left, feeling good about following my prompting, but feeling like I should have showed more interest in him. How easy it is to focus on one's own day-to-day problems and concerns—the simple administrative things—and not see the people around us.

That evening after dinner, I went back to the hospital and visited several patients. The member of our group that I had talked to earlier had just arrived at the hospital and was in my office. He told me he was a pilot, and as we talked I sensed that he was a little on the outs with the Lord. I just could not put my finger on my impression, but we continued to talk and I asked him if he would speak in church. He agreed to speak in sacrament meeting. Unfortunately he had just missed the church group that had come to visit the sick soldiers. Again there seemed to be something he really wanted to say. After some small talk about flying and medicine and kidney stones, a pilot's greatest fear, he told me about his story.

He was raised in California and always wanted to fly. He served a mission for the Mormon church and had attended Brigham Young University, and then, three years ago, was married in a Mormon temple to a beautiful girl from Texas.

He had been deployed a lot over the past several years, and during his last deployment his wife, who had been struggling with their religion, decided to leave the church. While he was deployed she had her name removed from the church records. Of course this caused him to question some of the things he had taken for granted. It also caused him to have to renegotiate the marriage contract he thought he and his wife had entered into in mutual good faith but that she had suddenly changed without his knowledge and against his wishes. In addition, she was now pregnant and in July would deliver his first child, a girl. He was not asking for advice. He had grown comfortable with staying true to his wife and being the father of his new daughter. He just wanted to tell me his story, and I was happy to listen.

Everything seemed to make more sense now, his attitude, his overall spirit. He confessed that he was weak from spiritual neglect and was now trying to be more diligent in prayer and devotion to his religion compared to when he arrived several months ago. In two weeks he will return home, back to the spouse he loves, and looking forward to seeing his first child. When he left I prayed that God would strengthen him for the rough ride before him. I also thanked the Lord for my wife and family.

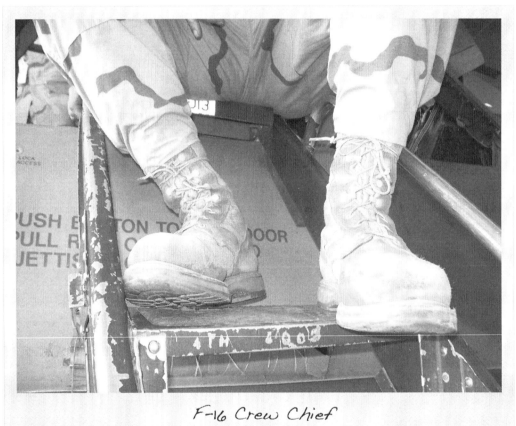

F-16 Crew Chief

—

# Chapter 35

# MORTARS KEEP FALLING

4/2/06

This week has been slow for adventure and exciting stories, so I will describe a busy but average day. This morning started with four mortars and an alarm red at about midnight. The mortar shells landed on the flight line near our F-16s. One of the members of our LDS church group is an F-16 crew chief and was only about fifty feet away from where two of the mortars exploded. He was unhurt, and when I saw him at dinner he said he would definitely be at church on Sunday. It is hard to get back to sleep after a mortar attack, and I waited to see if I should sleep on the floor for the rest of the night. If I can hear and feel the explosion then I usually pull out my sleeping bag and sleep on the floor with earplugs.

Figure 17. Large mortar shell that landed in the housing unit one morning between change of shifts.

When mortars land nearby they shoot debris about four or five feet high, which is why we sand-bag our trailers. The recent attack that landed a large rocket on H-6 housing shot fragments from four feet above the floor to the top of the trailers. If I were lying down all of the holes in those four trailers would have been just above my head. That small safety margin is why I sleep on the floor during mortar attacks. The earplugs are out of paranoia. A close blast can blow out your eardrums, so I often wear them at night, just in case.

Last night we had a stone patient admitted for surgery this morning, so I awoke at 0800 to go to the hospital. It was pouring rain, creating lots of mud and deep puddles. I negotiated the mud and puddles as best I could with my mountain bike and its wide fenders.

Figure 18. Neurosurgeon Hans Bakken shows damage caused in housing after an early morning mortar attack.

At the hospital we performed laser lithotripsy on the stone patient and didn't encounter any surprises. I then pulled two ureteral stents from other patients who were operated on last week. Just as I was going back home for a nap, a trauma patient was flown in. He had a gunshot wound to his back that had also penetrated his sacrum. He had blood in his urine, and we found a hole in his rectum, but no hole in the bladder.

Just as I was leaving, the ICU doc called to see if I could put a small chest tube in one of his patients to drain a fluid collection. Using the same techniques and equipment I use to get access to the kidney, I put the chest tube in and pulled out one thousand cc's of fluid.

Just as I was getting ready to leave, the Iraqi ward called and asked me to come over there to help with the placement of a bladder catheter.

Two days ago I went to the military car sales trailer and ordered a new 2006 convertible Mustang. All my kids wanted black with red interior. Military personnel receive a small financial savings of about $3,000, because the military doesn't have much overhead—just a trailer, no show room, or cars to test drive. Here you can order your car directly from the factory with all of the options you want, and then they ship to your home. We are in a war zone, and U.S. car manufacturers are reaching over here trying to get our hazard pay, and every other dime they can get their hands on, by selling new cars right on our military bases—in a war zone!

Later I received an urgent e-mail from Kris stating, "We saw a black and red one. It looked terrible. Don't get black with red interior!"

Consequently, I went back to the dealer to make the change, but he was out. An hour later I went back and made the change.

I broke my Sunday fast at 1730 hrs and went back to my trailer for thirty minutes of sleep. Just as I laid down, my pager went off. A patient was sick and had an enlarged scrotum. I rushed to the chapel to leave a note for my counselors to let them know I would not be at church. Then I hurried back to the hospital to attend the sick patient with the enlarged scrotum.

I explored his scrotum and found a large amount of stool inside. The bullet had entered his back destroying the sacrum and came to rest in the right scrotum. When a bullet enters the body it creates along its path a large cavity that sucks everything into the cavity. This bullet had sucked a large amount of stool from the rectum into the scrotum and the patient essentially had necrotizing fasciitis. I repositioned his testicles into the thighs and debrided essentially the entire scrotum and all surrounding devitalized tissue.

I was just getting ready to leave for home when the ER called to tell me the patient I had seen earlier in the week with a renal mass was back from Tikrit and was here for air evacuation. I had him come to the office, and I completed his paperwork.

I then made the rounds to see patients from the entire past week. All were doing well.

The afternoon conference session had just ended, so I called home and talked to Kris for my allotted fifteen minutes. Finally, I went home to write in my journal, print some pictures to send home with letters, read my scriptures, and went to bed at midnight.

Just an average day with rain.

Explosive Ordinace Disposal

# Chapter 36

———

# HE SAID SOMETHING ABOUT 'WATCH OUT' . . . BOOM

4/3/06

I readmitted the patient with the gunshot wound to the back and debrided more scrotum. It looks like the wound vac device worked. There was a lot of healthy tissue today where yesterday it looked like none. I tucked the testis back in the thigh and replaced the wound vacuum device which was working to restore vitality to the tissue. If it still looks good tomorrow, I will close the scrotum and see if the wound will heal.

Two mortars landed today during lunch. They must have been far away, because I did not hear them. Last week we received a patient who had been shot with a Hellfire missile just outside the base gates. He was spotted digging a hole for an IED with three of his friends, when the crew of the Predator saw them actually set up the IED, run the trip wire, and get ready to leave, they fired the missile. Two died at the scene of the crime, but one was alive. Even though the missile had landed in the hole, it did not appear to have detonated the planted bomb. The control command section for the Predator tried to relay the information to the explosive ordinance device (EOD) team rushing to the scene, but were not successful. When the EOD vehicles went out to secure the device, they drove over the wire and detonated the bomb. The entire event was captured by the Predator camera.

Poor communication could have cost them their lives, but that day they were lucky and survived.

One of the members of the Mormon service members church group is a Predator pilot and was on duty that night. He did not fire the missile but watched the entire scene on the monitor. When I told him about the patient who was found at the scene and sent to us but died of his wounds, he seemed surprised that I knew all about it and did not want to talk about it in public. That same day the whole story was in the local newspaper.

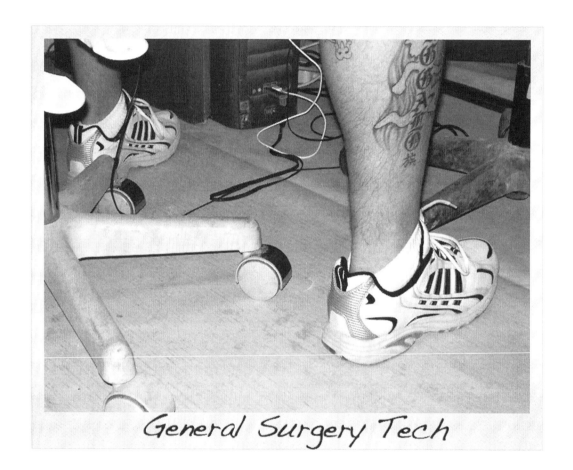

General Surgery Tech

# Chapter 37

––––

# YOU CALL THOSE THINGS TESTICLES?

4/3/06

Went to the gym for a work out. I have been working out everyday and really can not see a differ-ence. I have lost five pounds and am now down to a weight of 184, but I don't exactly see any bulk. I am definitely lifting heavier weights, but it does not show. I can see why so many of the troops are using steroids; they get big fast.

Of course when I examine their testicles in clinic and tell them that they are either on steroids, have used steroids, or smoked lots of marijuana in high school they look at me with prophetic disbelief.

"Wow doc, How did you know?"

Some will say, "You're right on both accounts. How did you know?"

Neither steroids nor marijuana makes you smarter.

Tank Mechanic

------

# Chapter 38

# I DON'T THINK MEDICS LAUNCHING MORTARS IS A GOOD IDEA

4/4/06

Major Hamilton is one of the commanders of the Army side of the Joint Defense Operations Command (JDOC). His office is responsible for the security of our base, Balad Air Base Iraq. He is a capable commander but has been haunted and taken out of duty by a three millimeter stone in his ureter down by the bladder, which is the narrowest portion and where stone usually gets stuck. His stone was stuck and he came to me is severe duress. I admitted him, controlled his pain with great doses of narcotics, but after two days he failed to pass the stone, and he needed to get back to work leading the men and women who protect the base, so I removed the stone with the ureteroscope and basket.

Figure 19. Large shipping containers filled with confiscated mortar tubes, mortars, guns, and rounds of ammunition.

The major has perfect military bearing and was stoic in the hospital. In appreciation for our services he gave me a unit coin and an invitation to visit him at the JDOC mortar brigade and motor pool. We worked out our schedule, and on the appointed day he was there to meet me, my urology technician and the nurse anesthetist who helped with his surgery. Even though we arrived five minutes early he already had his team prepared to show us several mortar tubes used to shell our base on a regular basis over the past three months. They had just been confiscated from insurgents within the last twenty-four hours. In addition, there was a large conex full of weapons recently confiscated, many AK-47s and thousands of rounds. Later in the week they would have even greater success.

After we touched and photographed the mortar tubes, we entered the JDOC operations center. Twenty-one large plasma flat-screen monitors hung from the wall. All were watching the four quadrants of the base with a J LENS camera capable of clear views beyond three kilometers, and of course perfect vision day or night. The radar units, C-RAM units, and Predator feeds were streaming live. The room was much like we are all used to seeing at NASA's Houston Space Center. The right upper screen was devoted to CNN live, and the left upper screen was used for continual sports feeds. There were four rows of desks, each equipped with computer, radar, and base maps. About twenty airmen manned the place. Every projectile larger than a .22 round gets tracked on the radar. Suddenly the room jumped to life and everyone instantly manned their stations. Precise nine digit coordinates were called out over the radio. The point of origin and the point of impact information was immediately relayed. Mortar teams were alerted at strategic positions on the base to wait for counterattack orders. The origin was five hundred feet off base. Simultaneously the J LENS scanned the area.

Near the north entry control point the convoys fire their machine guns before leaving base to make sure they are in working condition. A round from one of the guns had ricocheted back on to base and was picked up by the system. Everyone agrees and all turn back to chatting or other duties.

The Army Major's crew shared the same space with the Air Force. All of the information relayed between flights in and out and the ground forces on and off base are coordinated through the JDOC. When mortars fly into the base the system tracks the origin, looks for an intense hot spot, sends Predator or manned aircraft to the area of origin to constantly circle. The air traffic is determined and then commands for counterattack are issued. The fastest time to counterattack is thirty-eight seconds. If a counterattack can not be made within six minutes, there is no counterattack. The insurgent is not going to sit by his mortar tube for six minutes waiting for U.S. forces to show up. If we detect them fast enough air surveillance follows the vehicle or individual, and ground crews in the area immediately go to the site of launch to inspect for other tubes and mortars, which are frequently buried in the ground.

Major Hamilton directs us to a video monitor to show us background information on one of the recent patients who was sent to our ER but died. The J LENS picked up some suspicious activity on a road leading to our base, approximately one kilometer from our east gate. Three insurgents were shown digging a new hole in the middle of the road. After thirty minutes of digging with a pick and a small tree stump the hole was ready for the IED. One insurgent went to a berm and retrieved the IED, and another had the wire. All of this was seen very clearly on the J LENS at night as though it was bright and sunny. While the insurgents worked, a Predator had been launched and was watching overhead but unheard by the insurgents. Lastly the blacktop from the road was placed back into position and the IED pressure switch readied.

The Predator launched the Hellfire missile just as they finished their work and just as all three were standing together. They must have heard the whistle of the projectile because suddenly they became rigid and alert. The missile struck right between them with a terrific explosion. One of the insurgents had his legs blown off just above his knees but used his hands to scurry off into the brush. He traveled quickly about twenty yards towards a ditch. The second insurgent crawled out of the smoke, stood up, and ran to the brush. The third never moved.

Soon a three-truck convoy approached the scene. Major Hamilton yelled that they were going too fast, and the JDOC radioed for the trucks to stop before they got too close to the IED. There was no proof that the IED had been destroyed in the missile blast. The message didn't get relayed quickly enough but the first truck passed over the IED with no explosion. The second was not so lucky; it hit the pressure switch and detonated the IED despite all of the millions of dollars of high tech equipment, forty minutes of surveillance, and the use of a one-hundred-and-thirty-thousand-dollar missile. Miraculously, the turret gunner was knocked unconscious but was not seriously injured. The truck lost a tire and a front end. A Black Hawk was called in to search for the insurgent who stood and ran. He was quickly captured and still had a pulse. He was flown to our ER, but was DOA due to unsurvivable internal organ and large vessel injuries.

We went to the motor pool and secured a vehicle, and after a ten-minute drive we arrived at the north end of the base. There we were greeted by a tank mechanic who led us to an M109 Alpha 6 155 mm piloted Howitzer tank. After a tour of the beast, we fired it up. They apologized repeatedly for not being able to let us fire a few rounds; on base there is no room. The tanks purpose is really for base defense. When they take them outside the wire it ruins the streets and brings fear to the Iraqis. It is far more force than needed.

We each took a turn driving the tank around the yard a few laps. Then we got to stand inside the turret to move the cannon and spin it around. The tank crew showed and explained how the current range finders use sensitive computers to deliver each round on target, despite constant changes in barrel characteristics as the weapon is fired.

Figure 20. Lt Col Bishoff pilots an M109 Alpha 6 155 mm piloted Howitzer tank.

Our next stop was the mortar site. Around the base we had seen small encampments well covered from the road so as not to be obvious, and we had wondered about their contents. Once inside, we were introduced to the site for mortar return fire. When the Iraqis mortared the base, we returned fire with four to seven rounds. The direction of our return fire was calculated according to coordinates relayed from JDOC.

After explaining the system and showing us the technical equipment, the officer in charge offered to let us fire off a few rounds.

"To where?" I inquired.

"Balad City or the outskirts," he responded. "If we wait a few minutes the odds are really good that the base will take mortar fire, and we will return fire from here."

"But we could kill someone."

"That is the idea!"

"But we are medics and medics are non-combatants"

"Oh yeah, good point."

Four Star General

# Chapter 39

———

# HOW MANY MORTARS FIT IN A FIFTY-GALLON BARREL

4/7/06

Major Hamilton came in for a follow up on his metabolic stone work-up. After stone treatment we have the patient collect their urine for twenty-four hours, and then we send a sample via Federal Express back to Mission Pharmacal in San Antonio, Texas, for analysis. I receive the results by e-mail before the patient leaves the hospital and can prescribe medication, if needed, to help prevent stone disease. I received the major's analysis today so he came over to see what he could do to prevent a recurrence. He was unusually happy.

Last night his crew was on patrol four kilometers from the north gate near a branch of the Tigress River. A chopper had called in a suspicious activity on the river. Three Iraqi men were moving barrels in a barge. A squad went to investigate. They went in a boat up the river and secured the areas near the water. The barrels were just gasoline and the men were set free.

But there was a suspicious barrel near the water that appeared to be chained to another barrel submersed in the water. On land were several other barrels, all on the property of a wealthy sheik who had been on the major's radar for about a year. Calling out the metal detectors they started to find more and more barrels in the water and in the sheik's orchard.

When the squad finished they had almost one hundred barrels filled not with gas but with mortar tubes and five thousand mortars. It was the largest single cache of weapons captured to date in Iraq and right here in our own backyard. Very likely the supply of mortars used against us each day. The sheik was arrested and brought to his orchard to be photographed with the cache of weapons then sent to Abu Ghraib prison.

PFC Joseph Love

Photo: Judith D. DaCosta / Courtesy of **3CSC** Soldiers pay their respects at a memorial service for Pfc. Joseph Love, killed by a roadside bomb Sunday. (From Stars and Stripes, Mideast edition, Thursday, April 13, 2006 Reprinted with Permission)

# Chapter 40

———

# TODAY A SOLDIER DIED, HIS NAME WAS JOSEPH LOVE

4/9/06

Today is Sunday, and I went to the hospital to see patients and talk to a new Iraqi military patient admitted late last night after taking shrapnel to his back. His CT scan showed a large left distal ureteral kidney stone. I answered all of his questions and went back to clinic. I heard the usual trauma call and waited for the choppers to land. A few minutes later I wandered to the ER to see if there were any urology injuries, and to see if they needed a second set of hands in the OR. To my surprise, the ER was quiet, empty, and the techs were cleaning up the floor. I asked the ER doc what had happened.

"Open tib fib fracture, went straight to the OR, and the other one is in the morgue."

Apparently, just outside base, a squad on patrol early Sunday morning ran over an IED that destroyed the Humvee in which they were riding. The driver suffered the leg fracture. The front right seated passenger suffered bilateral lower extremity amputations, bowel evisceration, and upper arm amputation. He was dead when he arrived. No pulse, but still warm and still bleeding from his wounds.

As I turned to leave, one of the twenty year-old enlisted women from Patient Admission and Disposition (PAD) delivered the death papers to Dr. Varney for his signature, like she had many times before. Lacking any emotion at all, she was holding the dead soldier's ID card waiting patiently for Varney to complete his section. While he completed the paper work, I took the ID card from her hands and held it up close to get a look. It looked just like my card. He had used it earlier in the morning to eat breakfast before going out on patrol. He carried it in an armband holder just like I do. I don't know why I was surprised to see the card and to see how normal, how alive he looked. But I was taken aback, in a way fascinated that a healthy young man's life could change and end so suddenly. I looked at his picture. He looked very much alive. His eyes were not closed. I never met him but from the great big smile on his face he appeared to be friendly and warm, someone with hopes and dreams, someone with many friends, someone people like to be around, probably a bit mischievous. Now he was motionless and covered head to toe with a blanket. Time of death was around 1130 hours Balad time.

Somewhere, back in the United States it was about 0200 hours. Most people would be sleeping. But two men were putting on uniforms and would soon be going to Private Love's parents' home to knock on their door. That is the knock no one ever wants to hear, but the knock that all parents and family of those serving here are afraid will come. Joseph Love, private, United States Army, is dead.

Six days later the base paper confirmed what I saw from a quick look at Private Love's ID Card.

**Camp Anaconda soldiers pay respects to fallen comrade**

**Bronze Star is final tribute for GI killed by roadside bomb**

By Jeff Schoyol, Stars and Stripes
Mideast edition, Thursday, April 13, 2006
(Reprinted with Permission)

CAMP **ANACONDA, Iraq** —They came to say goodbye.

Many were choked up with emotion.

All were moved by the loss of Pfc. Joseph Love, 22, of Company B, 84th Engineer Combat Battalion, who was killed Sunday by a roadside bomb.

About 350 friends and colleagues gathered Tuesday at Camp Anaconda to pay their final respects to Love, of Sacramento, Calif. Among them was Spc. Richard Obleada, 33, who was in Love's convoy when Love was killed.

Obleada, of Virginia Beach, Va., said he remembers last seeing Love being put on a helicopter.

"I have to move on and get back in the game, like Love would have done," he said.

Obleada described Love as a man who lived life to its fullest and was fully committed to being a soldier.

"This guy was fearless. If you were to tell him to run toward oncoming traffic while blindfolded, well he'd have to think about it for a few minutes, but he'd do it," Obleada said.

He said he will always remember Love's smile and laugh.

Several of Love's friends mentioned they will also remember Love's sense of humor.

Pfc. Albert Tagoe, 24, said Love was an outspoken person, and that sometimes got him into trouble.

Once Love presented his weapon for inspection without cleaning it, said Tagoe, of New York. When Love's sergeant noted that the weapon was dirty, Love feigned indifference and said that it could still fire while dirty, Tagoe said.

"He paid dearly for his outspokenness that morning, but his weapon was never below standard again," Tagoe said.

Love's company commander, Capt. Andrew Marshall, said he had the privilege of twice promoting Love and looked forward to promoting him yet again.

Love always wanted to get into the action, said Marshall, 30, of Sacramento, Calif.

"That Private Love, always volunteering for something," Marshall said, choking up.

Love was posthumously awarded the Bronze Star, the Combat Action Badge and the Purple Heart, said Pfc. Angel Morales, 20, of El Paso, Texas.

Battalion commander Lieutenant Colonel Mark Toy called Love "one of the most dedicated soldiers in the battalion."

Toy also said Love's loss has affected him personally.

"I feel an enormous sense of loss in my heart. All the soldiers in my unit are my sons and daughters as well," he said.

Staff Sgt. Frank Johnson, Love's platoon leader, said he also felt like Love was family, calling Love his brother.

"My brother will never die. My brother will never be dead. He will always be loved in our hearts," Johnson said.

(Used with permission from Stars and Stripes, © 2006, Stars and Stripes. This reprint does not constitute or imply any endorsement, sponsorship of any product, service, company or organization)

Major General

# Chapter 41

---

# WHEN THE COMMANDER CALLS

4/10/06

This morning we had commander's call. This is what happens when important information needs to be officially distributed to the troops. The commander sets a time and everyone shows up. For the hospital it is done in two sessions so that everyone has a chance to hear the message, both the day and night shift personnel. This time the message was sweet music to our ears: going home.

I got up early, went to breakfast, at dining facility number 2 (DFAC 2) and arrived early for the meeting. When the ER team arrived they asked me what I thought about the active-duty lab technician from Abu Ghraib prison hospital who had been admitted last night with a scrotal and groin abscess. This was the first I had heard of it, which posed a problem, because the patient had been admitted hours earlier. If the patient had Fournier's gangrene, he could be seriously ill by now and well on his way to death. I decided to take a look. I put on my bike helmet and rode back to the hospital. This was also unfortunate, because it meant I would have to go back to commander's call in the evening. Attendance is mandatory and as usual, there is a sign-in sheet to prove your presence.

As I arrived at the back gate, I noticed that the plain unmarked van from the Special Forces compound was in the ER lot. They have two vans, a Range Rover and a Mercedes. Both have a darkly tinted inside window that separates the back compartment from the front. The vans, one is beige and the other white, have no markings on the side. It is interesting to me that they try not to stick out, but ironically, they are the only plain unmarked vans on base. The Special Forces' vehicles have been up-armored and built not to look any different. But on base they really stick out.

I walked through the ER to get to the ward to see the patient with the scrotal infection. The techs were wheeling a blindfolded patient back to the ER from the CT scanner with two SF guards, no identifying marks on the uniform, in tow.

"This one is for you, Doc," one of the medics said. "Shot in the pouch."

I followed them back to the ER and took a look under the covers. Sure enough a high-velocity round had entered the left thigh leaving a small hole. It exited through the medial thigh creating a nine-by-nine-inch gaping hole big enough to fit three large laparotomy surgical sponges with room to spare. Unfortunately, the blast effect of the exiting bullet resulted in an acute scrotum directly impacting the life, liberty, and pursuit of happiness for the left testis and part of the right, with the added challenge of missing half of the left hemi scrotum.

Indeed, it was a case for me. In fact most of the other surgeons were so concerned about the testis injury that they largely ignored the fact that he had a gaping hole in the inner left thigh. I suppose the lack of serious bleeding also helped them lose interest in the case. I informed the OR that I would be needing time for the case and then went the see the patient with an infected scrotum and groin.

He was the lab NCOIC for the Abu Ghraib prison hospital system and for several days had been dealing with an abscess on his right hip, which was infected with the feared Methicillin-resistant *Staphylococcus aureus* (MRSA), an organism that is highly resistant to most antibiotics. It had been drained in the OR, and he seemed to be recovering but then developed a new infection in the groin. This new infection rapidly developed into an abscess and also grew out MRSA. His wound looked stable, but was very painful to touch. I informed the OR of the need for another time slot to open and debride his wound.

The pager sounded to let me know the injured, guarded insurgent was in the OR. At the door stood not two but three guards to make certain the five foot Iraqi insurgent did not suddenly rise up, overtake the American-sized anesthesiologist, OR technicians, circulating nurse, and surgeon and flee outside the gate to Balad City or wherever he came from. Once he was safely asleep and intubated the guards retreated to the surgeon's lounge, where they could relax on the soft couches, read magazines, and eat Girl Scout cookies.

I debrided the insurgent's dead scrotum and dartos muscles layer and removed the bullet fragment from his scrotum. A Special Forces medic was there to assist me and to learn how to put a scrotum back together. He immediately identified the fragment as that from an AK 47 round. The center of the testis was gone; only the dense white tunical covering was left. I folded it back together and closed the tuncial dense covering around the testis, creating a small but palpable testis. I explored the right side and found a small blast injury to the right epididymis. The remaining scrotum was sufficient to cover both testicles and appeared relatively normal. General surgery was called to debride the dead muscle and explore the wound. They decided it was worse than they initially thought and that extensive work would need to be done, but I was done and moved on to the following case.

The next case was the patient with the groin infection and abscess. Some of the tissue was not viable, and several new small pockets of puss had formed. I debrided the devitalized tissue, washed out the wound and packed it for a trip to Germany and then home to Brooke Army Medical Center.

In clinic there were several patients with blood in the urine and one patient with a rare developmental anomaly called patent urachus, where the connection between the belly button and the top of the bladder did not involute or go away after birth, now manifesting as a large mass at the dome of the bladder. Once he was informed of the need for surgery, he begged for transfer to Germany, not because he wanted to escape from the war. He was not afraid of bullets, mortars and IEDs, but the sights, sounds and smells of the hospital had him more than a little unsettled. He was completely "freaked out" (to use his own term) by what he was seeing in the halls of the hospital. He refused to eat in the hospital cafeteria with all of "those sick guys." Later in the day, as I walked the halls and took a closer look, I tried to imagine how it may look to a nineteen-year-old Mexican kid who had come to the United States only two years ago and joined the Marine Corps just last year.

In the hospital, there were eight soldiers from a squad that took an IED blast. Most had facial lacerations, burns and swollen faces with plenty of open wounds to heal. Several still had black smoke on their necks and arms from the fire. The Iraqi ward was full of patients stitched up with staples in their heads stretching from ear to ear like a silver rainbow over grossly misshapen skulls where the bony parts of one or both sides had been removed. As I walked by them, I saw with fresh eyes and I wondered how really "freaked out" the young Marine would be to know that in each of these patients, half their skull was buried under the skin of their abdomen so it could be put back later—if they survive.

Major Lehr, the best nurse I have ever worked with, was yelling at Saad to stop moaning! Saad was in need of a pep talk. He was a patient from Iraq with very dark skin and bright white eyes. Compared to the other patients, his skin is so dark it appears almost purple in color, and his eyes so white that he looked ghoulish. He spoke and understood English well. He'd been shot in the abdomen and had been in the hospital for two hundred days. He has a tracheostomy and five enterocutaneous fistulas, holes in the intestine that drain to the skin, that kept him in the hospital. He was transferred to the ward several days ago and had been moaning and groaning since arriving there. Major Lehr had finally had enough of the noise and was explaining the rules.

"Saad, listen to me! How would you like it if someone was moaning and groaning, 'Ah… Ah ….Oh… Oh' in your ear all day long? You would hate it. And so does everyone else on this ward. You are going to be here for a long time, and we are all sick and tired of your constant groaning. Stop it, or I will moan and groan in your ear all day long until you stop! You speak English, so if you want something ask. If not, then just stop the groaning!"

I was wrong, and the Marine was right. This is a crazy place. The difference is that I am used to the trauma. His horrified reaction has served to remind me how abnormal it really is to be here. I filled out his paperwork and sent him to Germany for surgery to remove his urachal remnant. It will do him good to get away from all of the "freaks."

Later in the day I went on rounds to see all of my patients. As I walked onto ward 3, I immediately noticed a difference. There was Saad in the first bed on the left. He was wide awake, lying quietly, and listening to music. I waved. He smiled and waved back. Not a moan or groan to be heard.

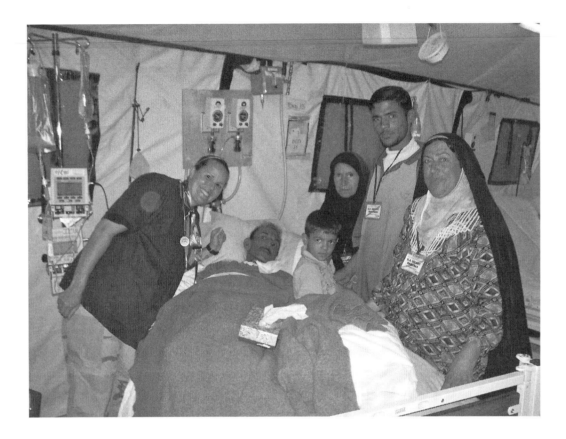

Figure 21. Major Lehr, Saad with family members at his bed side.

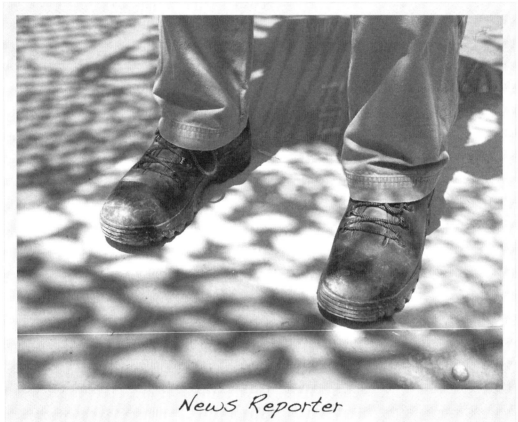

News Reporter

# Chapter 42

———

# AVERAGE DAY TWO

4/11/06

We took Patient 1037 back to the OR to debride more of his dead leg muscle and replace his wound vac. I put a drain in his scrotum to help with some of the edema. Randy Beamer, from WOAI-TV in San Antonio, Texas, was here to do a story. He was accompanied by Dewy Mitchell, the public affairs officer from Wilford Hall Medical Center. Their purpose was to experience and report on "an average day" in a military hospital staffed mainly by San Antonio locals.

In their honor, local insurgents staged a live mortar exercise, intermittently launching four mortars. To give them a real feel for the average day, the mortars activated alarm red, which sent us scrambling to the cement bunkers outside the tent hospital. I was at one end with a group from our clinic. The Iraqi patients, en masse, were at the other end of the bunker surrounding Randy and Dewey. As the mortars exploded near the hospital I took pictures of the Texans and their anxious faces as the Iraqis babbled in Arabic while staring at the two minorities in their midst.

Figure 22. Dewey Mitchell with camera and Randy Beamer with video recorder in the bunker during code red.

The mortars stopped, and the all clear sounded. We went back to work.

In clinic I saw Iraqis and Americans with severe medical ailments: testis cancer, severe urethral stricture after pelvic fracture, blood in the urine also called gross hematuria, herpes, recurrent urinary tract infections and stones. After a busy day I was ready for a break. I went to my trailer and laid down. I was going to stretch before going out for a run but was soon fast asleep.

The night patrol, which consists of a pair of F-16's and several Predators, leaves base at dusk to fly around the area looking for badness, harm, and ill intent. I have been trying to catch a video of the F-16s taking-off at dusk with their afterburners blowing and the sun setting. One night while out for my evening run near the flight line but without my camera, I saw this very image and was impressed. Since then I have been running with my back pack and camera, ready for a repeat, but the fighter pilots are expert at varying their routine, which means that I would have a difficult time capturing the moment.

I stirred from sleep with some hunger and a bit of confusion as to where I was exactly. I looked out of the trailer to see a beautiful sunset, grabbed my back pack, and went for a three mile run. Just as I reached the corner near the flight line, I heard the thunder of an F-16 taking off and immediately thought of the impression I had had twenty minutes earlier. Too late, no camera in the bag. But, oh what a beautiful sight to see, two F-16s blasting off, full after-burners roaring and the sun just setting. It was still light enough to catch perfect images, but I was not prepared.

After a leisurely run over the three-mile course I went back to the trailer to shower and to change. I felt like eating Indian food so I went to DEFAC 3(dining facility) for Indian night. Several Indian patients had invited us to their camp for dinner, and we had enjoyed fantastic chicken curry, mangos, and rice, all simple but perfectly tender and savory. On Saturday I went in search of more Indian food for lunch. I found it at the DEFAC 3, but it was mediocre at best.

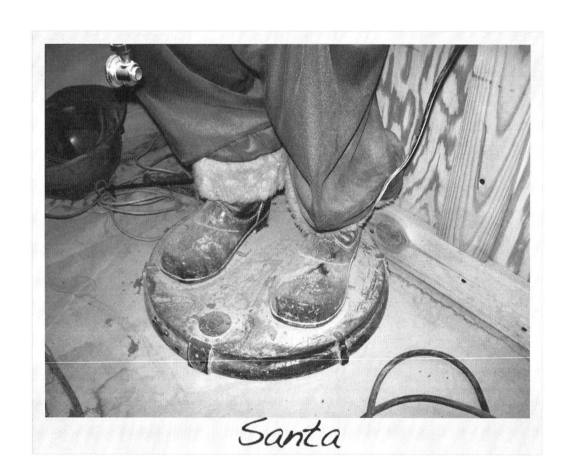

Santa

# Chapter 43

------

# IN NEED OF SPIRITUAL NOURISHMENT

4/11/06

Twice a year, October and April, the Mormon church has a general conference, which is broadcast worldwide for all to see and hear. We tried to get a simulcast from the internet on base so that we could watch the conference sessions. Many letters and requests were submitted, and it looked promising. But at the last minute, the idea was shot down by computer security. They deemed it too risky to have streaming video on computers in Balad. Since the airing of the April conference, one week ago, I have been anxiously waiting for the talks to be posted on the LDS website. Tonight, as I returned to my trailer, I had a very strong impression to go back to the hospital and read the talks, especially those from the Priesthood session.

It was with significant anticipation that I loaded the site and was thrilled to see that the talks had finally been posted. I started with the first talk of the Priesthood session "See the End From the Beginning" by Elder Dieter F Uctdorf. The messages were fantastic and as I read the second talk a palpable feeling of peace and protection filled the tent that was my clinic. I read the next talk, and the next.

Alarm red sounded. I jumped under the desk and grabbed my body armor. I had just finished the Priesthood session with "The need for Greater Kindness" by President Gordon B. Hinkley and had just started his Sunday morning talk, the one that sounded like it might be his last. I dearly wanted to finish it. So adorned with my vest and helmet I returned to the desk and kept reading. Mortars continued to land in our vicinity shaking the tent, accumulated dust from sandstorms covered the desk and computer. In the air there was a subtle dust cloud adding to the entire effect. The lights in the tent swung eerily back and forth, dangling by their Velcro straps, having been disturbed by the blast from a mortar landing nearby. Despite the alarms and sirens, I was at complete and absolute peace. It felt like there was a literal bubble over my area, and for a short time I relaxed in the peace and comfort of God himself.

I ignored the second and then third incoming warnings and continued to read. Normally I would have already been back in the bunker, probably with Randy and Dewy, but I could not pull myself away from the powerful messages of the April 2006 conference, and I felt perfectly safe and sound. There was an unmistakable presence of comfort and peace like a large protective shell had been created overhead. I finished reading most of the talks given at the conference, and as I finished the all clear sounded. I then sent an email to my family telling them of my experience and asked my oldest son Brandon to read the Priesthood talks, which could be a big boost to him.

Public Affairs

———

# Chapter 44

# NEW EXCUSE FOR 'I AM LATE BECAUSE . . .'

4/12/06

Kidney stones are so common here that we are trying to reach out to the different units to discuss hydration, prevention, and warning signs. Sergeant Wilson from public affairs had scheduled an appointment for an interview from which she intended to create an instructional DVD. At about 1200 hours she called the clinic to inform me that she would be late.

What else do you really have to do? Was the thought that came across my pessimistic mind. That negative thought was interrupted by the truth. Sergeant Wilson called to report that she would be late because a mortar shell had just landed outside their building and had not exploded, at least not yet.

"Had it exploded, it may have been better for all of us because we could leave the building—that is, if we were not injured. But now that the mortar had not exploded, they had to wait inside until EOD could disarm it."

How odd, I thought, that they had not evacuated the building; instead they were locked inside. Anyway, she would be late for our appointment to discuss a short video on kidney stones, diagnosis, and prevention. I went to the gym to go for a run. After an early dinner I went back to the hospital to finish up some work, and to see the patients for the evening.

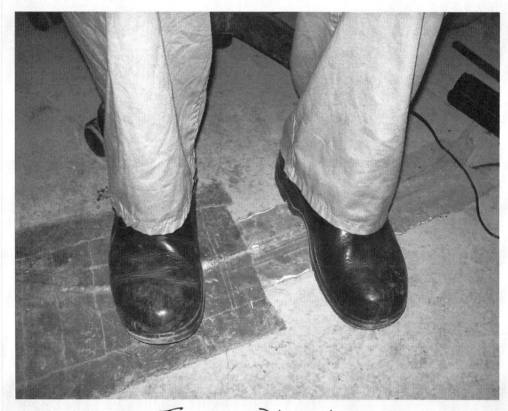

Trauma Director

# Chapter 45

————

# MASS CASUALTY

4/12/06

The day started out quietly and then suddenly, with only ten minutes notice, the ER was abuzz with activity. A mass-casualty disaster had occurred in a nearby town, and we were alerted to prepare for victims. A suicide bomber blew himself up in the middle of a busy town square just as evening prayers were ending and the filled-to-capacity mosque emptying.

An official announcement said there were approximately forty dead and thirty critical patients coming to us. Everyone who was present changed into scrubs and waited.

First one helicopter, then another, and more waiting to land, the sky seemed to be filled with choppers. The first Black Hawk landed handing off two patients: an obese Iraqi male with blast trauma to head and face, and a boy thirteen or fourteen years old with blast wounds to the chest. Someone had already placed a chest tube. He was awake, scared, and seriously injured. I wondered where all the other surgeons were. It was about 1900 hours, and no one had returned from dinner.

Lieutenant Colonel Jeff Bailey, the trauma chief, came to the ER and started to help with triage. Two more choppers landed, and now there were five patients in the ER. One was confirmed dead by several ER techs who reported no pulse and body temperature same as room temperature. The body was quickly moved to the morgue, simply because more bed space was needed.

Next to the dead Iraqi was another victim severely burned on his face, arms, and abdomen. While two more patients were being settled into our overflowing ER, I realized that I had not been personally notified of the mass casualty situation because my pager had not been activated. I had simply been walking through the ER routinely visiting patients before leaving the hospital for the evening. Bailey, the trauma chief standing next to me, did not get a direct page either. This was a simple oversight with significant consequences. Someone had neglected to send the mass casualty page to all personnel. We called the command section and had the page sent. Seconds later all of our pagers sounded, and now the number 911 would appear on every display. More help should be on the way. Two more patients arrived in the ED.

I took the kid, mass-casualty patient 2 (MC 2). He was intubated by one of the nurse anesthetist while I placed another chest tube and had him taken to CT for a scan. I turned to the patient with the hole in his chest and inserted a right-sided chest tube while the nurses put in the left tube. Off to CT for him. I was then summoned to look at MC6, who had a large hole in his pelvis which was streaming a combination of dark red blood and urine.

The ER was now full, fifteen patients in total. Most of the staff were busy putting in lines, drawing blood, giving blood, taking films, and moving patients. A Hollywood producer was there taking in all of the real life drama and trying to stay out of the way. He came here to experience this new type of warfare with the intent of creating a modern-day *M*A*S*H* TV series using the 332nd as the backdrop. He and his camera crew were all over the place filming and trying not to miss anything.

I hurried off to check on the young man's chest films and CT. The chest x-ray revealed he had accumulated a large amount of blood in his chest, but the drain tubes were still in good position. The x-ray showed a large piece of metal overlaying his heart. The CT scan revealed its true location. The chunk of metal had entered from his back and was now lodged in the ninth thoracic vertebra of his back, sitting inside a transected spinal cord. He was administered two units of packed red blood cells and was stable for now.

Bailey sent me to the OR to help a general surgeon explore a patient's abdominal injuries. The nurses and surgeons had been unable to place a bladder catheter. He was prepped, and I helped drape and move him to make room for another patient in the same room. One of the commanders, Colonel Gary Arishita, was also there.

The general surgeon looked up at me and said, "Hey Bishoff, are you going to steal the case from the colonel?"

I was puzzled by the question, but replied, "No, Bailey asked me to come here and help you explore this guy."

Colonel Arishita immediately recognized the need for organization and went to see Bailey to get a new assignment.

Since I was sent to put the bladder catheter in and to help explore the abdomen I ignored the general surgeon who was unable to place the catheter in the first place, put on some extra lube and it slid immediately into the bladder. No injury. The general surgeon seemed offended at that and at the idea that I was going to open the patient's belly while she worked on gaining venous access in the groin. She took the scalpel from the tech and made the incision. The patient had a few bowel injuries, but minor stuff.

The rooms were blasting hot air to keep the patients warm. Cold patients become acidotic and coagulopathic. Cold, bleeding patients die. The room temperature was about one hundred degrees, and inside our gowns we were about ten degrees hotter. Despite the heat we were focused and working quickly. But something was filling my gloves, and my hands were pruning like a water-logged kid in a swimming pool. The surgeons, nurses, and techs were soaking in sweat, which dripped down our legs, and filled our shoes. Drops from surgeons' foreheads were wiped with sterile towels that were then tossed into untidy piles all over the floor.

Lieutenant Colonel Bailey came into the OR and redirected me to another room to explore the patient with the large hole in his pelvis, which was pouring blood and urine from the hole in his side. He was asleep and being prepped. Lieutenant Colonel Dave Powers, the oral and maxillofacial surgeon, was already there to help.

We opened the patient's abdomen and packed his liver and spleen. No major bleeding. In his pelvis there was a large hole in the bladder, posteriorly. I opened the bladder to get a better look inside and found only the one hole. I closed the bladder and placed a suprapubic tube. Next we carefully inspected the bowel, where we found multiple serosal abrasions, which we over sewed. No major injuries.

The commander, Colonel Taylor, wandered into the room and informed us that we had received twenty-one patients total. Two patients died after arriving, and two died on the way. The rest had significant injuries and would need multiple operations.

We closed our patient and moved him to the ICU just as Bailey brought in yet another with bladder and scrotal injuries. I moved to the area where this new arrival was being explored. I closed his bladder and reconstructed his testis and closed the scrotum. The OR was beginning to slow down. Some of the patients had major orthopedic injuries but could wait until later to come to the OR.

To say we were drenched would underestimate the amount of sweat soaking all of us. We had to empty our shoes between cases. All of the OR staff were soaking wet—hair, hats, top, bottoms, socks and shoes. Ocean-wet better describes those of us who had been in the OR for the last four hours with no relief.

A palate of Gatorade and one of Red Bull had been placed outside the OR doors and were quickly consumed. The cooler that was almost always full was now almost empty. It was now 0430 hours. Would anyone else in the entire world ever understand how hard we worked or how much we cared about the unfortunate injured Iraqi military and civilians who had the great fortune to be transported to the 332nd?

The heat and flurry of activity of the busy morning had exhausted me, and I was ready for sleep. I was too tired to change into my desert camouflage uniform which was mandatory—scrubs out of the hospital forbidden—so I simply collapsed onto the exam table in the urology clinic. Even the down-blast rotor wash shaking the tent of the urology clinic and the aircraft noise from the landing zone could not keep me awake. After only an hour, I woke and decided I needed the comfort of my bed and trailer. I climbed into my uniform and peddled my bike back home. The bed felt better than I could ever remember. I checked the mattress, but it was the same as all the other nights. I felt fifty pounds heavier as I became one with the mattress.

What seemed like only seconds, but was about an hour later, the alarm sounded and it was 0040, the start of yet another day. The feeling of being numb immediately took me back to how I felt every three days during the first two years of my residency. Being on call every second or third night, working thirty-six hours a shift and being told "if you do this stuff enough when you are almost unconscious, it becomes second nature." Despite being exhausted, you must be responsible because you are on call. A flood of memories and emotions came back to me as the warm water hit my face, and I rejoiced that I was a urologist and the in hospital call of general surgery was behind me.

No change in the total count at morning report, but a lot of tired faces were in the group sitting around the commander's table listening to a recap of the night's activities. We discussed each patient in detail, but there was some confusion. Patients had been assigned mass casualty numbers in the ER, but our friends in Patient Admissions and Disposition had changed their mass casualty number to admission numbers.

I went on rounds to check on the patients from the morning. All of those with urology injuries were stable and all had clear urine—a urologist's delight. Every patient's kidneys were functioning, and clear urine was coming from the proper place.

The clinic already had new patients waiting. There were the usual problems: testis pain, kidney stones, and frequent urination. A steady stream of patients came and went.

In the early afternoon I went to see all of my hospital patients again. Again all were all doing well. I had four patients on the self-care ward waiting for transportation back to their forward operating bases. They were all abuzz about the mass casualty from the prior evening. As it turned out, one of the Marine infantrymen was a nurse who had been called to active duty as an infantry grunt from the reserves. He had recruited personnel from the self-care ward to help with the mass-casualty emergency. They volunteered, working all night, moving patients, changing dressings on horrific but not life-threatening extremity wounds, helping the ER staff place chest tubes, dressing third-degree burns and even open fractures. They had all worked throughout the night and were now just waking up and processing the evening's events by talking about their experiences. I was happy to listen to what they had experienced. This was a fresh perspective, one long forgotten, to look through inexperienced eyes. Eyes that had never seen the horrific devastations of a mass casualty, eyes that had not yet seen traumatic wounds of any kind, eyes attached to minds that did not want to actually think about the reality of war. Being in this situation was exactly what they feared most when they were deployed to this war zone.

Despite their fears, and without being asked, they had done an incredible job helping to ease the pain and suffering of Iraqis who looked very much like the enemy they had been sent here to fight. The words of these men on paper are far less dramatic and moving than actually looking into their faces and hearing the fear in their young voices as they retold the stories of the wounds they had helped care for. They are Marines, infantry, and cavalry. They are the tip of the spear at the front of the line of injured soldiers. Now they have seen what could possibly lie in their own future as soldiers on the streets, at the doors, next to the Iraqi people, and very much in harms way. Instead of moving away from it they charged forward to help, to volunteer, to do whatever was needed.

I listened to their stories and realized that they needed to be recognized. I invited them back to my office, and one by one I wrote letters to their first sergeants or commanders detailing their help with the mass-casualty situation and closing with the statement that their actions brought great credit to themselves, their units, and their branch of the service. They were thrilled, so I printed two copies—one for the first shirt and another to send home to their moms. I promised them it would make their mothers so proud they would cry.

I was now exhausted but decided the best thing to do was go to the pool and swim. It was only 1730 hours, and I knew I could not fall asleep in the pool. I swam about a mile and was just beginning to feel refreshed when my pager urgently beckoned. A new kidney stone patient was in the ER. I biked back to my room to change out of my wet suit.

Before I could get there my pager sounded again. This time 911 was displayed— another mass-casualty situation. Apparently twenty Marines had been injured by a mortar attack. Mortars leave terrible injures. Lots of small fragments embedded deep in tissue, all tissues, all over the body simultaneously. Surgeons, nurses, techs all waited together in the ER and outside on the landing pad, waiting for some of our own to arrive, and anxious to give them the best care they could receive anywhere in the world right here in Balad.

We were exhausted from the activities of the evening, but excited to help in any way necessary. Next the word came that our intensive care units were too full to take the Marines. They would fly over us and go on to Baghdad at the 10th CSH. The mood immediately turned to disappointment. Despite the events of the last twenty-four hours, despite the fatigue, there was not a single person in the hospital who did not want the chance to care for and possibly save the life of even one of our Marines.

All of the surgeons piled into the team truck and went to eat dinner. It was Thursday, which means Mongolian barbecue at dining facility 3. It was the usual dinner; too much food to eat. Our pagers went off. Two Marines with head injuries were coming to see the head-and-neck team.

In the ER there were two Marines from the mortar attack. One had head-and-neck wounds; the other had a severe chest injury along with liver and kidney damage. This information came from the brief transfer summary from the exploratory laparotomy performed at the forward operating base of injury. The problem for me was that the victim's bladder catheter had been occluded with blood. I put in a hematuria catheter and irrigated one liter of dark blood and clots from the bladder.

I found the surgeon of the day (SOD) and informed her of the need for a CT to evaluate the hematuria. The SOD's assessment was that the Marine was too unstable and that he needed to go directly to the OR after resuscitation with fluids, blood, fresh frozen plasma, platelets and factor seven. The patient needed to warm up to correct his coagulopathy. An anesthesiologist was working to keep him stable as blood, and not just a small amount, was draining from his chest tube. After two and one-half hours, he appeared stable. He was warm and his coagulopathy had resolved. When the body is trying to stop major bleeding it will empty all the stores of clotting materials. When they are used up, the bleeding continues unabated and the patient bleeds to death. The lungs don't have blood to move oxygen to the muscles, and muscles without oxygen stop, including the heart. This Marine was young. His heart was strong. He was stable, but was still bleeding from his chest. The call team all talked about what to do next. It was decided, or so we thought, that he needed a CT to evaluate his liver, lungs, and kidneys.

I had to retire to the clinic to rest because it was now 2000 hours, and my two hours of sleep had run out. I was not stable. Just as I fell asleep the "incoming" alarm sounded. I got on the floor of the clinic, but was so tired I decided dying would not be so bad. I also realized that the cot was still one foot under the level of the sand bags surrounding the tent. I quickly calculated the risk and decided it was not much greater on the cot than under it, but the cot was much more comfortable. I struggled back up on the cot and tried to sleep. Incoming sounded again. I turned over and covered my eyes with my arms to protect my vision. Incoming. The mortar sounded close as it landed with a boom, shaking the tent walls.

Next came the more serious alarm red warning, which means you need to get your helmet and vest and take shelter in the bunker. I had been in the bunker so much this week, and there was certainly no place to sleep there, that I decided to stay in the clinic. I remained on the cot and covered my eyes a little tighter. I had already tried to sleep in body armor, and it was not comfortable. If it was my time to die, then it was my time to die! I was really too tired to care. I just wanted the CT to get done, to hear the all clear signal, and to go to bed.

Finally the all clear came across the "big voice" across our sector of base, and I rose and went to see the patient's scan, but no scan had been done. I went to the ICU and the patient's bed was empty.

"Gone to the OR an hour ago, just before the alarm red," said Major Long, a neonatal nurse from Wilford Hall.

I went to the OR where two surgeons were exploring his chest for the source of bleeding. They had decided to forgo the CT and visually explore his chest. He had a large right-sided incision deep into the chest, and they were struggling to see the injury. They did not listen to sound advice about the CT, so they certainly would not be asking for any help. As I walked through the surgeons' lounge, about 0200 hours. Bailey and Bowers simultaneously asked why it was taking so long to get the scan.

"What scan? They decided they did not need it and took him to the OR because he had blood coming from his chest tubes," I said.

There were moans and groans as all had been waiting to see the results of the scan. We knew they had made a big mistake. We were all discouraged and left at the same time to go back to our rooms and leave them to fight the battle they had mistakenly chosen to fight through an incision that would not get them to the root of the bleeding.

I showered and took out my contacts. Once again the bed was perfect, as I sunk deep into the foam at 0300 hours. Being in bed this early would give me a priceless four hours of sleep tonight.

No sooner had I closed my eyes than the pager sounded with a call to operating room 1.

"They opened his abdomen and they need you here right now," sounded the nurse.

"Are you kidding me?" I responded as I hung up the phone.

I was certain the bleeding was from the liver or kidney, and since they were calling me it had to be kidney. The surgeon of the day was supposed to be a good liver surgeon and would not be calling if it was the liver. I only wished they had called four hours earlier, after the CT had shown the problem to be in the abdomen and before the patient had once again depleted all of his coagulation products and was again bleeding to death.

I put my contacts in, rode my bike back to the hospital and entered the back clinic door. In the clinic I have a stash of laparoscopy equipment including vascular staplers that can be used to quickly and securely divide the arteries and veins of the kidney during laparoscopic surgery. On several occasions, I have used them for traumas to remove kidneys and have been impressed with the result even while working in a large pool of blood with only hands to feel the planes, find the vessels, and place the stapler.

On the back table there were piles of laparotomy sponges all soaked with blood. I donned my headlight, gown, and gloves. There was a large hematoma in the abdomen, and nothing was recognizable. There were packs around the liver, over and under, and the colon was reflected. Blood was welling up from the right abdomen from the area where kidneys normally reside. I used my hands to find the kidney, open the fat around it to feel the surface for injury. The kidney was blown into several large pieces from a metal fragment that snagged a hole in my left glove. Blood was welling up faster than we could suck it out with two suction tips. I glanced toward the head of the table to see Dr. Stormo quickly pushing more blood, platelets, and any other blood product he could get his hands on into the patients IV. There was a stack of twenty-five to thirty empty blood product bags at his feet.

My fingers found the top of the kidney. There was a large complex injury to the entire upper pole of the kidney, which was essentially in pieces. I quickly called for the stapler and mobilized the kidney to the vascular pedicle. With one squeeze of the handle the kidney was freed, removed and the bleeding almost completely stopped. There was some small oozing from the liver and the chest wall, but finally the patient's source of misery was gone in an instant.

I could not hold my anger in any longer.

"Too bad we did not get the scan a few hours earlier, like we had discussed," I said.

"The blood looked like it was coming from the chest," she responded.

One of the surgeons had scrubbed out to see other patients in the ER but was looking over my shoulder now.

"Why would that have helped us in any way?" she quipped.

"Almost eight hours ago, American surgeons looked into his abdomen and told us about the liver and kidney injury. We never addressed them until right now. And we could have known about this many hours ago and many units of products earlier."

"Oh," she said and left the room.

The other surgeon and I packed the liver and did a temporary closure of the abdomen. I was surprised to hear him say we needed to roll him over and close the chest, which was being held, closed temporarily with towel clips. After struggling for over two and a half hours to solve the bleeding problem though his chest, they quickly closed with towel clips and opened the abdomen.

He stabilized overnight and was taken back to the OR the following day to over sew the liver injuries and to close the large diaphragm defect. In the afternoon he was stable enough the get a flight to Germany—alive.

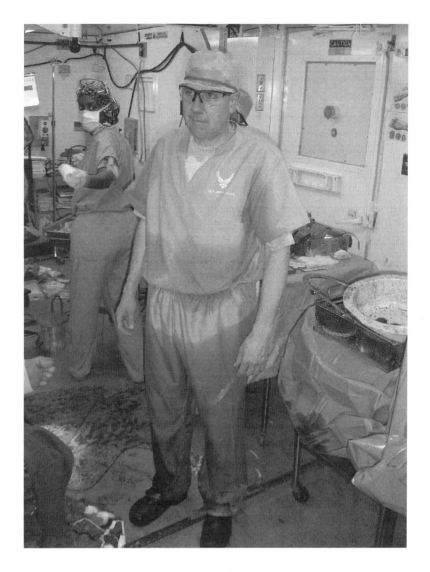

Figure 23. Lt Col Bishoff in operating room #2, soaked in sweat and tired after operating all night during mass casualty.

Female Pilot

# Chapter 46

## FOD AND FOD PULLERS

4/15/06

We have a small LDS service members church group who meet each Sunday for Sacrament services, to sing hymns, and to hear faith-promoting talks by our own members. Church with weapons is a new experience. M-16s and 9mms on the chairs and on the ground is not a sight you usually see at any church service, but it occurs regularly here for all faiths. In the Mormon, or LDS, service-members group we have a large portion of our group made up from an F-16 squadron from the Hill Air Force base in Ogden, Utah. Using only members of our LDS group, we have one of everything needed to man our own F-16 squadron: munitions expert, weapons expert, egress expert, crew chief, and a female F-16 pilot. That is enough to fly one of these jets.

The crew chief and egress systems technician invited any interested in our group to visit the flight line. Early in the week the urology tech and several patients who had been treated for stones and were waiting to return to duty went to the flight line for an F-16 squadron tour. We met the squad at the gate and drove to their workshop.

Figure 24. Sign at entrance to the flight line.

One of them brought out two silver pieces of aluminum with a dull hook cut out of the end. They were about six inches long and three inches wide. Both were numbered and marked "FOD puller." Now this caught my attention. I had never seen a FOD puller and had no idea what the term FOD meant. As the most senior office, I normally would have made a mental note and waited for the holes to be filled in before asking questions. But my interest in these simple pieces of marked and numbered aluminum that seemed so essential to the mission had to be explained now. So I inquired about their purpose. All of the enlisted members gave me the same uncertain look. Uncertain because they were not sure if I was serious.

"What is FOD and FOD pullers?"

The crew chief responded, "You'll see, sir."

The truck drove over a large cattle grate-like piece of metal on the road and stopped. We all got out and FOD pullers were handed out to all crew members.

"All the rocks have to go from the tire tread all the way around," ordered the crew chief. Not wanting to be left out and having a sense that there might be some resentment that the lieutenant colonel did not do his share, I pulled out my Leatherman and started digging rocks, lots of rocks, from the truck tires. The ground in front of each tire was swept, the truck pulled forward and all remaining rocks plucked from the tires. Now we were ready to see the planes FOD free.

FOD, meaning "foreign object debris" is anything not properly attached to the plane that could get sucked into its engines and bust apart the turbine fans, which would result in complete destruction of the million-dollar motor in a matter of seconds. If FOD is sucked in, the plane is usually destroyed, and occasionally the pilot if he or she cannot exit in time. All tools including the FOD pullers are numbered and each tool has a specific place in the box so that all can be accounted for before leaving the area and before the plane is ready for takeoff.

Sergeant Joe Leman was the crew chief. He took us to his plane. He had just washed it and cleaned the inside. He knew just about everything about it. He pulled up the maintenance ramp and then the crew ladder and let us inside. One at a time we held the stick and closed the canopy and took pictures. I was surprised at how child-like I felt. I caught myself dreaming about being a fighter pilot just like a ten or twelve year old. Suddenly I was thinking about how it would feel to actually fly the F-16, not just to close the canopy. You know thumbs up and salute to the crew chief, throttle down, taxi out, full throttle and afterburners, and straight up just like the real pilots do all day long here in Balad. In the seat of the F-16 you feel suspended in air. You can't really see the nose or the wing looking straight ahead. I was a kid again with new dreams. Forget the surgery dream, that is old stuff; this is new, exciting and better.

Figure 25. Lt Col Bishoff in cockpit of F-16 contemplates a career change.

Wait, what was that. "Hey, let someone else have a turn." I could barely hear with the canopy closed. We were all kids again. I wonder if pilots ever dream about taking kidneys out through three small holes. Probably not.

Lee Greenwood

# Chapter 47

---

# EASTER SUNDAY

4/16/06

We admitted two insurgent patients from Abu Ghraib prison last night. Both had kidney stones, and we added them to the OR schedule for this morning. I paged the urology tech, but got no answer. We sent a runner to his room, but he was not there. He was either at breakfast or running. We started to set up the operating room, but orthopedic surgeons decided their case was more urgent and bumped us.

We finally started the first case at 1200 hours. The first patient had a left-sided pelvic kidney (a condition where the kidney is not in the back under the ribs, but never developed as usual and was sitting low in the pelvis) and narrow ureter with anatomy that was anomalous and difficult to negotiate with the scope and laser fiber. I tried but could not advance the scope and had to place a stent and stop. This presented a problem because he came from Abu Ghraib, which meant that he would to be under constant guard and surveillance during the week his ureter dilated, and we could come back and try again.

Having had a ureteral stent myself (two weeks during my own stone experience in 2005) I can assure you that no translator in the world would be able to convince the insurgent prisoner that we were not purposely torturing him. He would certainly go back to Abu Ghraib and tell his five hundred buddies at the prison camp, "The Americans tortured me using a mysterious device they surgically implanted inside of me. Every time I urinated the device gave a strangle hold on my kidney. Next, after two interrogation trips to a room the Americans call an operating room for a fake condition they call kidney stones; they let me go back to prison."

The second patient had a large two-centimeter stone that broke easily with the laser, but lasing the stone created about one hundred pieces that needed to be removed. Two hours later I placed his stent, put the lid on a bucket full of stone particles, and moved him back to the ward.

The ICU team called about a former Iraqi patient with a scrotal abscess who had been operated on during the mass casualty several days earlier. He had urgently been moved out the night of the mass casualty. When we got him, we put him on the schedule, drained the abscess created when a gunshot went through his sacrum, into his rectum, and finally into his scrotum.

Yet, today was still Easter Sunday, and between all of these patients I had church services to conduct as the LDS service-member group leader. I had prepared a talk and was actually looking forward to concentrating for at least an hour on our Savior and the importance of Easter.

It was already 1800 hours, and the day nearly done. I rushed back to my room to shower, and then have a quick dinner. The dining facility had been decorated for Easter using elaborate vegetable sculptures; nothing about Christ, just bunnies and bright Easter treats. Steak, shrimp, ham, lobster and crab were the main entrees. Large displays of carved fruit, cakes and decorations were all about the room. It was busy. Many had come to enjoy Easter dinner in Balad.

Figure 26. Easter celebration at dining facility number 2.

At church our Stake representative gave a talk from the most recent world training seminar. It had nothing to do with Easter. This I deemed strange indeed. His ten minutes turned into twenty-five. Jay Metcalfe, my counselor, gave his talk, which was about Christ and about Easter events that changed our physical and spiritual worlds. His words were humble, simple, and powerful. I shortened my remarks, but we still ran over time by five minutes.

After church, two of us gave a blessing to a young enlisted man trying to get his life in order for his return to the United States. I laid my hands on his head and paused for just a few seconds. The room seemed to grow brighter, even with closed eyes, and the windows of heaven opened giving me a clear view into his life. Words flowed to my mind and to my lips, specific words, details about him as a father and husband, also not so flattering words of warning, and advice and counsel straight from a loving Heavenly Father. I touched on details about goals he had set and yet had done nothing to accomplish since coming to Iraq. Intimate pieces of this soldier's life filled my mind. I admonished him to be at church each week and to be faithful in reading the scriptures each day, then closed the blessing. With tears in his eyes, he turned around and looked up at me.

"Wow, you don't even know me. This is scary. How did you know everything about my life?" he asked.

"You are right," I replied. "I don't know you, but God does, and I am just here working for Him."

"Darn straight you are!" he spontaneously blurted out, catching himself before swearing in church.

Finally, back to the hospital, this time not to see patients, but to call home. On Sunday I call home because it is the only time I can talk to my family. When I first arrived in Iraq, I tried to call often, but rarely if ever was able to reach anyone. Today was Easter, and I really wanted to talk to my family. On days other than Sunday, I had tried to call Kris, at least fifteen times on her cell phone, and never reached her, not even once. When I did catch someone at home it was either too late and they were tired or off to bed, or it was just before soccer, piano, scouts or many other things.

I called home for Easter. Kris seemed a bit down. The girls were fighting. I tried to talk to Maddie, but she continued to scream for Lauren to hang up the phone. After getting my ears blasted for the fifth time, I asked to talk to Tanner, then Brandon. Soon my fifteen minutes were up. Easter Sunday was over. I read Luke 22–24 and went to bed.

NFL Cheerleaders

# Chapter 48

———

# CIVILIAN CONTRACTORS SALARIES, WORTH EVERY DIME UNTIL . . .

**4/18/06**

Today was an uneventful clinic day; no interesting cases, just more routine testis pain and urinary frequency cases. After clinic I went to the gym with Sergeant Sechler, my urology teammate. It has been good to have a workout partner about the same strength as me. At times our workout results seem to have been frustrating to him because I am fifteen years older but can lift about the same weight and seem to have an edge on the aerobic exercises—running and swimming. Sechler chooses to continue smoking, making it difficult for him to keep up on the runs and laps in the pool. I cannot and never will understand the habit of smoking. Tobacco smoke stinks, causes severely disabling disease, takes much of the smoker's money and eventually kills the smoker. It is a product developed under lies and distortion, yet millions senselessly continue to support the tobacco industry by giving them at least three to five dollars a day. I fully understand the nature of nicotine addiction, but smoking is void of any redeeming qualities.

After clinic I went back to my room to work on my personal history. I was interrupted by a page from the ER. A Jamaican contract worker with the civilian military contractor KBR was injured in an IED attack followed by small arms fire. From the IED blast he suffered a severe pelvic fracture. I was called because he had blood in his urine. He initially went to CT scan but became hypotensive and unstable. Instead of CT he was taken directly to the OR.

He had multiple intestinal injures and a gunshot wound to the back and flank. There was a large hole in his kidney at the renal hilum, which is the area where the vein and artery enter the kidney. He also had massive bleeding from the flank wound and from the renal vessels. I tried to mobilize his kidney, but it was inseparable from the psoas muscle. Clearly, he had previously had surgery or shock wave lithotripsy for stones or a prior kidney infection. Whatever the cause, the result was the same. The kidney was stuck and almost impossible to mobilize from the surrounding muscle. Severe bleeding was in the process of slowly ending his life.

I took a large pair of curved mayo scissors and cut away part of the psoas muscle with the kidney specimen. This allowed me to elevate the kidney, secure the artery and vein with a large statisnky vascular clamp, use scissors to divide the artery and vein, and stop all of the bleeding. The vessels were then over sewn with prolene suture and the clamp removed. The major source of bleeding was stopped, but the pelvis continued to bleed. We packed him and sent him to the ICU. I went back to bed. The day ended at 0100 hours Wednesday morning.

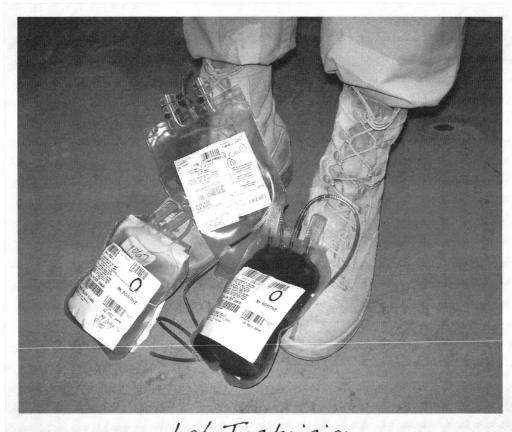

Lab Technician

# Chapter 49

———

# A FEW GO HOME

4/19/06

The patient from last night went back to the OR at 0500 hrs with uncontrollable bleeding from his pelvis. After 120 units of blood, platelets, and FFP he died.

There was a squadron breakfast meeting to say farewell to the head-and-neck team. They are Army surgeons who, after serving for six months in Balad, will be leaving to return home. Their replacements have already arrived, and there is a new spirit of enthusiasm in the voices of those going home: Eugene Ross, ENT; Roy Cho, EYE; Bret Schlifka, Neurosurgery; and, a nurse anesthetist and an anesthesiologist.

There is another neurosurgeon, Hans Bakken, who was in private practice when he became aware of the Red Cross Neurosurgery Assistance Program in Germany. Due to a shortage of neurosurgeons, civilian neurosurgeons were invited to Germany for a two to three week rotation to help with the care of our troops. Hans left his private practice to take one of these rotations. He met Warren Dorlac and Tye Putnam, two Air Force general surgeons stationed in Germany. They impressed him with their personalities, skills, and especially their dedication to their patients. He was impacted to the point that, despite no obligation to the military, he joined the United States Army. After officer training they sent him here to Iraq. He had enjoyed the Army and has been enthusiastic about the surgery here, the care we are able to deliver to all patients, friend or foe. He is also fascinated by all the weapons available to the military. He received permission to carry an M-16 as his weapon, instead of the 9mm most other officers carry. He recently volunteered to extend, from the six months normally served by the Army physicians and nurses, to a full year.

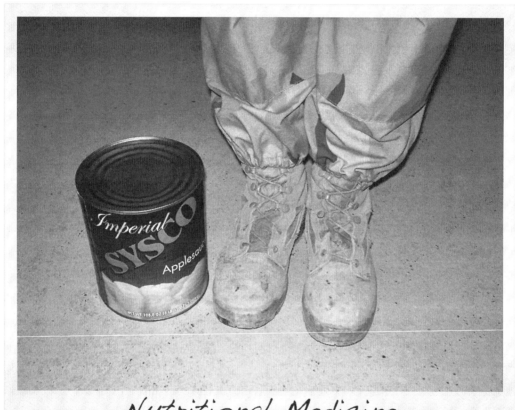

*Nutritional Medicine*

# Chapter 50

---

# WHO WANTS TO RIDE WITH YOU

4/19/06

Today after the Army surgeons' farewell breakfast and photos, I returned to find the clinic waiting room full, and all were waiting to see the urologist. They had the usual problems: testis pain, frequent urination, blood in the urine, and kidney stones.

I asked one Marine what was the wildest thing he had seen. He proceeded to tell me a story about being in six different Humvees when they were destroyed by IEDS. Seems he has only been here for six months and has already ruined six Humvees.

"Wow, I bet no one wants to ride with you!" I said.

"Oh, no, Doc" he returned, "Everyone wants to ride with me. Six blown trucks and no one injured, except for some incredible ringing in the ears. Everyone wants to ride with me. I have the best record in the unit."

Some people have lucky boots and some people are just lucky. God bless those men with continued good luck.

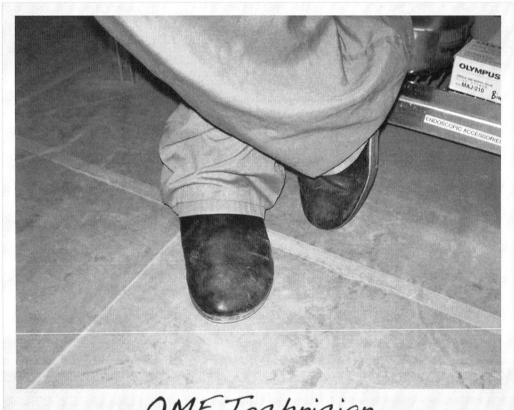

OMF Technician

# Chapter 51

---

# JUST LIKE THAT THINGS CHANGE

4/20/06

More stone patients, and more patients with testis pain. One stone patient is a contractor in charge of personal security for one of the Three-Star Army Generals. His wildest moment? Being fifty feet in the air with the general when their Black Hawk lost power and crashed back onto the pad.

The next stone patient said his wildest moment happened eighteen months earlier. After a patrol in a small city outside Ramadi, his squad stopped to rest. They positioned themselves inside a small cement courtyard with a wall about four feet high. He had just taken off his helmet when a car stopped and tossed a hand grenade over the wall. Before anyone could move there was an explosion followed by small arms fire. The grenade knocked him out. When he woke up, he was under fire and being dragged into the house by two buddies. His head was bleeding from two areas and his ears were ringing, but he was alive and aware enough to know he was injured. He pointed to the two scars on his head, one small one on the front forehead and a longer one about four inches toward the back of his head. Both were clearly visible. The scars on his head have healed, but the memory keeps him fearful everyday, knowing that in just seconds your life can be forever changed.

One of the OR technicians is specialty trained in oral maxiofacial surgery. She married her high-school sweetheart, who is also on active duty. They don't have children, but each have a Harley motorcycle. She has pictures of him on her desktop and on the walls of her room. She talks frequently of trips they have planned to take together when she returns home. Her husband is in physicians assistant school with the Air Force. Before he went back to school, he was often away on temporary duty out of town as was she,  so she was looking forward to getting home and being home while he attended school.

She was one of the technicians on the head-and-neck team caring for the many patients with severe head injures from motor vehicle accidents and gunshot wounds. A few of them died in the OR, even while she helped the surgeons do everything in their power to save them.

Figure 27. Armored vehicles destroyed by road side bombs towed to the bone yard at Balad Air Base, Iraq.

Late last night the first sergeant knocked on her door to inform her that her husband had just been in a serious motorcycle accident and was in the ICU at Wilford Hall Medical Center, San Antonio Texas, our home base with a life-threatening brain and head injury. He had been declared brain dead, but they would try to keep him alive while she worked her way home to be by his side.

Her boss had just learned two days ago that his wife had a positive biopsy for breast cancer and would be having surgery next week to perform bilateral mastectomies.

Both of them took the first flight out of Balad this morning at 1000 hours. My tech and I put our clinic on hold to help them move their belongings out of their rooms, pack their bags, and mail them back to the States.

We went to the Base Exchange to purchase a foot locker for their things. Several of the security police forces that were with us in Qatar were in the exchange buying food. This seemed odd, since the food was free and in great abundance. I joked that they were forced to patrol and buy food. They seemed awkward and then told me that they had been buying food for some of the third-country nationals (TCN) who came from different countries to get lucrative jobs cleaning and doing laundry. As Iraqi nationals, hired to be day laborers on base, they could not get food for themselves, at home or on base.

Much to their surprise, we bought the food for them. I was deeply moved. Here were two junior enlisted kids whose job it is to guard the TCNs to make sure they don't try to harm us, and even with their very meager pay as airmen, they were in the exchange buying food for TCNs who did not have enough to eat. This was just one touching example of the spirit of compassion that I have seen in many of the American soldiers. These young men represent the future of our country, and while I once had great doubts about what the future holds for our country, I no longer doubt. This also represents a spirit of service, compassion, and kindness that will not likely be seen in the press back home.

Supply

# Chapter 52

_____

# IED INJURY BUYS YOU A BALAD SPECIAL

4/22/06

More kidney stones and minor testis complaints today. I returned at midnight to see an Iraqi police officer injured in an IED blast. You could not find two square inches of his skin that did not have a hole from dirt, rocks, or metal fragments. He was treated with the Balad special, which is having four or more surgeons operating on the patient in one trip to the OR. First, the left eye required debridement of two metal fragments and closure. We would normally operate at the same time as the eye surgeons, but there is a problem with the OR floors. We have three operating rooms that are mobile units designed for rapid deployment and set up. The problem is that there is no drainage in the floors, which are usually soaked with blood, irrigation fluid, or water. Over the past two years the floors have rusted out so they are weak and unstable. Simply walking can cause the whole OR floor to move. When the eye surgeons are working under the microscope, it makes it essentially impossible to see, so the eye team goes first.

After the patient's eye was closed, the ENT team started their work with bilateral neck explorations of the major vessels as indicated by the findings on CT scan, which showed fragments in the area of the carotid arteries. While the head-and-neck team worked, I helped the general surgeons explore the abdomen. The patient had several small bowel perforations that were easily repaired. The bladder had a rupture and required opening, repair and placement of a suprapubic tube. The abdomen was closed. I moved to the penis, which had a fragment hole in the urethra and another in the corpora of the side of the penis. Once they were repaired and the destroyed penile tissue removed, I opened the scrotum to fix a ruptured testis. Finally the orthopedic surgeons came to realign the broken tibia and fibula on the left leg and to re-explore the right arm, which required opening from the shoulder to the hand to repair all of the vessel injures. Thus one Balad special served up to an Iraqi policeman unfortunate enough to suffer the same injury as thousands of others but lucky enough to be alive.

Comics On Tour

# Chapter 53

———

# NO ONE WORKS ALONE HERE

4/23/06

Two stone cases today. Nothing new at work. Went back to my room after rounds and surgery to sleep. After three hours of blissful dreaming, I was awakened by a page to the ER.

A twenty-two year-old tank driver and gunner had just returned to the unit in his Humvee when the compound was mortared with seven rounds. The first landed near him. He had just removed his body armor. A fragment entered his back almost midline. He was awake and moving his legs and feet. A CT scan showed midline entry and the immediate split of the fragment from the middle to the right chest wall and through the kidney stopping just under the liver. The CT showed that the kidney had a deep laceration with some bruising but minimal urine leak. We could observe the injury for now. He remained stable overnight, asking about when he could skateboard and go back to driving his tank—the two loves of his life. I believe there are now three because he has a new love: life itself.

His commander came to visit him and then sought me out. The Army liaison knocked on my door and stated that two soldiers were looking for me. In walked a lieutenant colonel and a sergeant completely covered in body armor, shoulder plates, knee pads—real soldiers from the tip of the spear. The sergeant had a completely tip of the spear, up-armored M-4 with his finger in the ready position but lowered once they entered the room and realized it was clear. Just one doc in scrubs, pretty safe. The lieutenant colonel had his M-9 in the holster. Off came the gloves and the officer introduced himself and shook my hand. There was the immediate and unmistakable feeling of a unit coin on the palm of my hand. As he shook my hand he thanked me for the careful and excellent care I had given to one of his boys.

"We are from the forward operating base Palawalta, and we get attacked daily. Our unit has seen a lot of damage. When we hear that our guys have been transported here, we all feel a lot of relief because we know that they are going to get great care. We want you to know that we appreciate all you do. It is a great honor to have you here to support us and we wanted you to know that."

The sergeant echoed the sentiments.

I did not even operate on this patient, so I felt awkward about taking his coin, but took it and accepted the compliments for the entire 332nd. No one works alone here. All I could say was that it was our pleasure and honor to be here for them. They put their gloves back on, walked out of the door and straight to the Humvee convoy parked in the lot. Time for work.

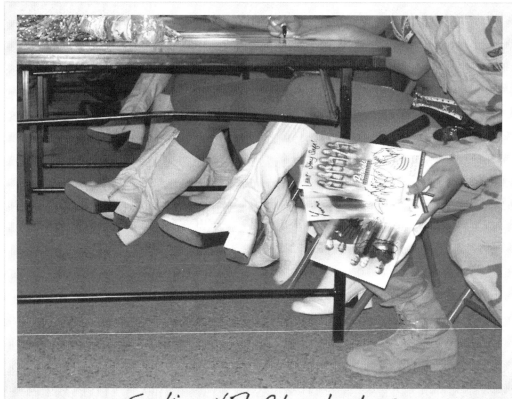

Seeking NFL Cheerleaders

# Chapter 54

_____

# THE FRESH AIR OF WORSHIP

4/23/06

I grabbed a quick dinner and hurried off to church. Sunday services are a welcome break from the day-to-day activities that make every weekday just like the others. The scene over here is remarkable compared to a regular Sunday back in the United States, or anywhere for that matter. Most of the church members have weapons they carefully place under their seats. Desert camo uniforms or official issue physical training (PT) shorts and T-shirts are the only thing that the active duty can wear. The civilian contractors wear Levis or shorts. Most Sundays the speakers are wearing PT gear including shorts. Nevertheless, the Spirit is strong.

The talks and testimonies are true, simple, and pure. Many new members, recent converts, are present. They are honest. They are not full of canned phrases and words but tell their feelings and ideas freely. I am convinced that the future of the church is in the young adult who, at an age of understanding, studies the gospel and receives personal revelation that the church is true. These young people suddenly realize how wonderful, how powerful the gospel is in their lives. Like the scriptures describe, they feast on the words and wonder how they or anyone else could function and live without them. Uncluttered by the culture of Mormonism, they live the gospel and share their newfound life with everyone who will listen. Today a young airman gave a talk about the Priesthood. After thirty-five minutes, I had to remind him about the time.

He simply said, "After researching this topic and getting myself ready to receive the Melchizedek Priesthood, I am so excited that I just can't stop thinking or talking about it."

There is a new contractor who showed up today. He came in late and did not take the sacrament. During the Sunday School hour he asked good questions about the need for the Holy Ghost and wanted to know the difference between the spirit of God and the Holy Ghost. I had the distinct impression that he may have been there to disrupt and to cause many to question their beliefs. I am anxious to see how this plays out over the next several weeks.

We have two new members who are talented in music. One plays the organ and the other is gifted in vocals. It will certainly add to the overall spirit of the meetings to have them here with us. Sunday—the best day of the week.

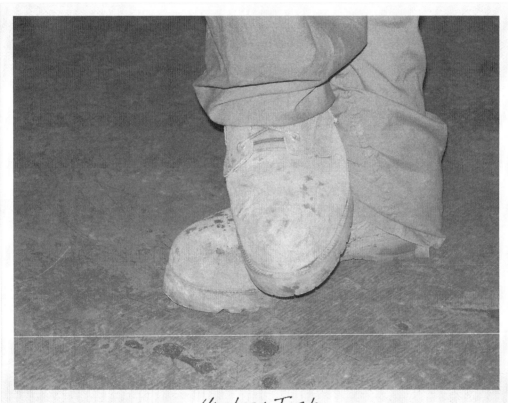

*Urology Tech*

# Chapter 55

———

# PLEASE DON'T KICK THE BAGS

4/25/06

Today the helicopters brought us two Marines who had been on patrol in a small city thirty minutes by chopper from Balad. Their squad was clearing a former school, once full of elementary school children and teachers but was now empty or used by insurgents. The two Marines had been searching the school, moving up a staircase to clear the upper rooms of the building.

In Iraq, it is common to see cloth bags that Iraqis use to carry and store things. They are also used as sandbags or dirt bags for protection. They are everywhere. You see them lying in the streets and in buildings. They are cheap and have many different uses.

So the Marines were not the least bit surprised to see such bags in the school. While they were walking up the stairs, the Marine on the right kicked a bag with his right foot. Unfortunately this bag instantly exploded, tearing off a large part of his foot and leg and sending fragments into his arms, face, and eyes. The Marine on the left was spared most of the blast by his battle buddy, who took the brunt of it. Unlike his buddy, he only sustained fragment wounds to the lower left leg, singed facial hair, minor face burns, and several small fragments to the penis.

I cleaned the less wounded Marine, washed his face, peeled back the burned skin, and fixed the holes in his penis while the orthopedic surgeons dug out fragments from his legs. They will both be on a plane to Germany in the morning.

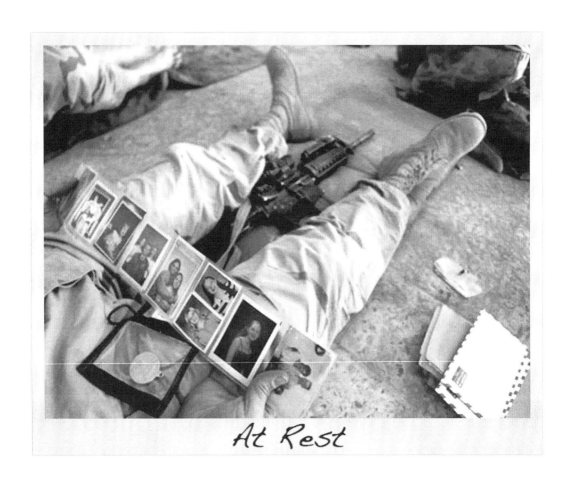

At Rest

# Chapter 56

———

# SOUL MATES

4/25/06

I have only listened to a few stories about love and meeting soul mates that have been worth remembering. The first one I heard was on a National Public Radio Valentine's Day special. A caller related driving through Chicago on a trip from Indiana with his family as a young man about eight years old. In a suburb of Chicago he saw a small girl about his same age in the front yard of a home sitting on her bike. She had long black hair. He was struck by her and watched out his side window then looked out the back window until she was out of sight. His sister commented and teased him about it for the rest of the trip.

As he grew up, the memory of the girl with black hair sitting on her bike would often pass his mind when back in Chicago, and he often passed by the same house going to visit relatives. He eventually went to college. I think he went to the University of Indiana. One day he spotted a young woman with short black hair near the student union building. There was something special about her that caught his attention. He eventually met and married her. After being married for about twenty years, they were driving through Chicago on the way to a funeral. He drove past the house and remembered the whole scene from many years earlier.

He turned to his wife to say, "Remind me to tell you a story about that house" just as she said, "Oh, look that is the house we lived in when I was eight."

Today I saw a patient who was twenty-three, and when I asked him if he had any prior surgery he said, "Just a vasectomy."

"What?" I said, "A vasectomy? Why does a twenty-three year-old get a vasectomy?"

"Cause I already got three kids, and, Doc, I don't know if you have any kids, but trust me, three is enough!"

He then went on to tell me his love story. He was born at the county hospital in a small town in Alabama. He was best friends with a guy named Paul. They were close and are both in the same Army unit here in Iraq. When he was in high school, he was at Paul's house and met Paul's cousin. He said that when he first met her something just clicked and there was a feeling like he had seen her before. But the town's population was only about twenty thousand people, so everyone seemed familiar. Right after meeting, they found out that they had the same birth date and year. They fell in love and married.

When his wife became pregnant with their first child, his mother pulled out his baby pictures. It was a quiet Sunday afternoon and they were speculating what the child might look like. There was his picture in a close-up of him in the nursery with his name tag clearly visible on the picture.

"Oh my God, look at that" his wife suddenly said, pointing to the basinet in the nursery right next to his. She pointed to the one with the pink blanket, and, of course, the pink name tag with her name on it. Soul mates. He told me the story had kept them together through some "really hard times, like being away in the military for years at a time."

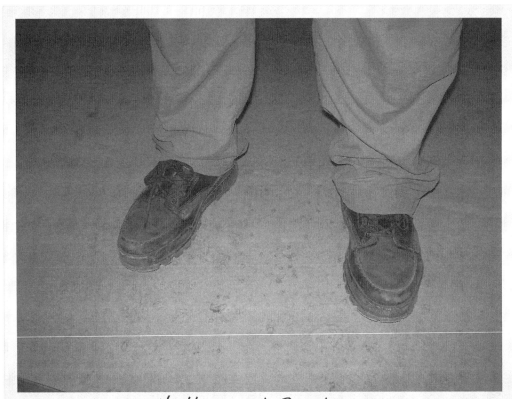
Hollywood Producer

# Chapter 57

———

# WHO WILL MISS IT?

4/26/06

Today I saw a JAG officer for some minor testis pain complaints. We did CT scans of his kidneys, an ultrasound of his testicles, and blood and urine work. He kept asking about the pain. I gave him a four page handout on testis pain that I wrote for this very purpose, so I don't go crazy saying the same thing all day long.

To distract him I said, "It must be really interesting practicing law here. What is the wildest case you have prosecuted?"

Then he told me this story. The Army unit in his area had just received several five-thousand-dollar Honda power washers. Last year I had bought a power washer and tried to get my kids to start their own business washing driveways. The business part with the kids did not work out, but anyway I have a nice three-hundred-and-fifty-dollar power washer. I use it about once a year to get the brick patio clean from the messy birds that visit our back yard.

The Army's power washer cost the government $5000 and had a stand, trailer, water tank, motor, and hoses. It wouldn't fit in the back of our Suburban.

Apparently, one of the soldiers got an idea, probably inspired by the recent re-release of the Johnny Cash song about stealing a car from the factory one piece at a time so that he could send it back home in small pieces. He took a torch and cut the washer's frame so it would fit in boxes, then started sending parts of the power washer home. Somewhere along the way someone in the shop became suspicious and started asking why a soldier would cut up the frame of a new power washer. One thing led to another and the case was solved. The punishment? Return the parts and take an honorable discharge from the Army. In other words, he leaves Iraq and the Army scot-free.

Secretary of the Army

# Chapter 58

_____

# IS IT WORTH THE EXTRA CASH?

4/24/06

This war is famous for many reasons. We have superiority in the air, on the ground, in equipment and arms, but we can not stop the insurgents from sniping, bombing, and mortaring us. Media coverage follows forward troops as the war is unfolding. We are spending record sums of cash that are flowing out of our country faster than oil is flowing out of Saudi Arabia. In 2008 we were spending 7.3 billion dollars per month. We have given a lot of this money to contract companies that provide services for the war effort.

KBR is the prominent civilian contractor in the gulf. They are paying civilian workers up to two hundred thousand dollars a year to do dangerous jobs here. At least once a month someone comes to the hospital with a story that says the money was incredible until a single event, then suddenly it did not seem like enough money. Last month we heard the story from a contractor from South Africa pulling in two hundred thousand dollars. It seemed like great money until a sniper shot him in the cervical spine rendering him a quadriplegic.

This month the contractor-casualty was a truck driver. He drove the big rigs that bring us food, water, and almost everything else. The trucks often originate from Kuwait and are on the road for long periods. Normally that would not be a problem, but here there are a lot of road hazards. Tonight his convoy was hit with an IED that disabled the trucks, stopping the convoy and exposing them to a barrage of small arms fire. A bullet hit my patient in the left hip, fracturing his femur and blowing his urethra in half at the base of the scrotum and stopping near the testicle. Orthopedic surgery fixed the femur with a temporary external fixator. We opened the abdomen, then the bladder and passed a catheter from the bladder into the urethra and tied the two together to get the catheter into the bladder. Then I was able to put the urethra back together. He will leave for Germany tonight on a military air evac plane. Then the military will fly him to the States.

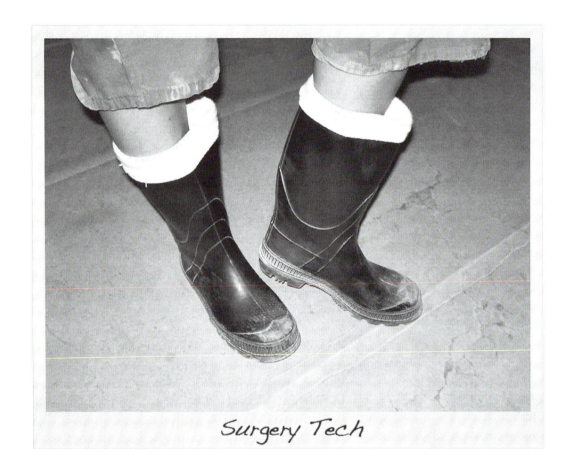

Surgery Tech

# Chapter 59

———

# HAVE YOU SEEN MY SON? HE IS ONLY 12

4/26/06

Recently we had several patients transferred to our hospital from Baghdad. Details were not precisely conveyed along with the patient. Apparently there had been a vehicle-borne IED detonation in the city with many injured. Several civilians sustained severe head injuries and were sent to the 332nd, including a twelve-year-old boy. Initially, he was taken to the 10th CSH in Baghdad and then forwarded on to Balad because we have the neurosurgery team here and the boy was found to have a head injury.

Imagine being this Iraqi boy and suffering the trauma of an explosion, waking up in a strange hospital with Americans everywhere. Imagine the grief of his father searching a war-torn mangled city and country, struggling to find his son in the area of the explosion, in a war zone with check points and danger at every turn. Was he dead? Was he alive? Where was the medical city? 10th CSH U.S. Army hospital? I am sure there were sleepless nights and constant fear as the father searched, wandering from hospital to hospital asking about his son.

I was not on the boy's case, but apparently he recovered well from loss of consciousness. He had a depressed skull fracture with a large laceration that was treated by the neurosurgeons. Soon after, he was extubated and moved to the ward. He could not remember the exact address of his home but was confident that he could find it if he was allowed to return to Baghdad.

After the boy had been on the ward for almost twenty-three hours there was a call from the north gate. A man from Baghdad was there looking for his son. The boy was not informed, just in case it was not his father. The man was picked up and escorted to the hospital. He urged his escorts to hurry him to the ward. When the man saw his lost son he ran to embrace him, and his son ran to be embraced. Tears flowed not only from the man, but from his son and most of the team in the ward. The father's mission was complete; he had finally found his son and was taking him where a twelve year old belongs—home.

Congressional Aides

Chapter 60

_____

# ROCKET-PROPELLED GRENADE

4/29/06

Today I saw a first sergeant who was a platoon leader from Ramadi. He had blood in his urine so I sent him for a CT scan and did a cystoscopy on his bladder. His work-up was negative; there were no significant findings. He probably had IgA nephropathy, which is a kidney condition that allows the kidney to leak blood into the urine or it may be due to his sickle cell trait. He will be fine.

I asked him about his Iraqi experience.

Apparently last week, he was involved in a complex attack with mortars, small-arms fire and rocket-propelled grenades (RPG). Most of the team, in one of several trucks on patrol, had gotten out to return fire. Only the gunner, "One of my Joes," he said, was still in the truck when an RPG entered the back right window, injuring the gunner and setting the truck on fire. The squad extricated the gunner and quickly put out the fire. The truck seemed drivable so the first sergeant and a buddy jumped in and headed for the FOB. About two blocks later they were hit by an IED, and the back of the truck caught fire. Small-arms fire followed. With the truck still burning, they somehow managed to get to their forward operating base. Once inside the gate, away from small-arms fire, they finally put out the fire, which had burned close to the ammo containers in the back.

60 Minutes Producer

# Chapter 61

_____

# WHEN 60 MINUTES REALLY DOES SHOW UP IN YOUR OFFICE

4/29/06

Solly Granatstein, a producer for CBS's *60 Minutes*, came looking today to find pieces for a news story. It makes everyone a little nervous when the press is in the hospital. It seems they wanted to do a story about the physicians, but who knows for sure. Granatstein brought a DVD with a story he did on medics who went to Thailand to help after the tsunami last year. Apparently it was a strong, positive story that became a hit. It was obvious the he hoped to follow-up with a similar story here.

I met him briefly in the hall being escorted by the public affairs (PA) team and had a chance to ask them for the missing piece of my *Boots of War* poster — a strong picture of dead soldiers' boots, M-16s, and helmets. They said they had exactly what I needed. I was thrilled. My project may see print.

Well, later in the afternoon, just as I was getting ready to leave, the *60 Minutes* entourage came to talk. I told them several of the stories included in this journal and some additional urology unique experiences. They were very interested and started writing and writing, story after story. Almost two hours later it seemed they had heard enough and deemed me worthy to have an interview with the anchor. I recognized his name Scott Pelley, the youngest of the group with *60 Minutes*.

Hospital Vice Commander

# Chapter 62

———

# CALL ON THE SECRET PHONE

5/2/06

This afternoon I was suddenly paged to the command section. Dr. Gary Arishita had received a call from the 10th CSH in Baghdad about the U.S. deputy ambassador to Iraq, who was in their hospital with a large left-sided kidney stone and severe pain. The irony and the problem was that the 10th CSH does not have the means to treat a stone of this size in the ureter, except for open surgery, which would be considered "not within the standard of care." The irony? The Army fought the Air Force and insisted that it was not a good idea to have a stone laser and "fragile" ureteroscope in the battle field on the front lines.

I was offered and, of course, excited to accept the case. We have been trying to get the Army to understand the importance of having the standard ureteroscopic and laser equipment necessary to treat kidney stones. We have become the center of excellence for treating kidney stones here in Iraq. For me, it is a great thing to have all the necessary equipment, but for other urologists it is frustrating to have spent six years in residency training and then not be able to use those hard-won skills. Equipment is necessarily limited in a war zone where one small bomb costs more than all the equipment needed to treat kidney stones.

The deputy ambassador was on a helo headed for Balad. About an hour later, word came that he was arriving. Major Guillory with her team from patient admission and dispositions went to meet the chopper, like they always do. Two choppers landed—gunships with machine guns on the side. The door on the front chopper opened and out jumped two heavily armed guards who immediately took position on one knee ready to fire. Two more jumped out and moved to the narrow opening from the helo pad leading to the hospital. Once it appeared clear, they signaled to the others and four more surrounded the deputy ambassador and escorted him to the hospital. Now Major Guillory had asked the second two off the chopper if she could help them find the place they were looking for, but they ignored her and moved forward, so Major Guillory and her personnel returned to work in the PAD. The ambassador, surrounded by his heavily armed entourage was left outside lost, surrounded and waiting for help.

I came out of the clinic to greet them and moved the patient to my office while two soldiers guarded the clinic door. Before he arrived I had searched for information about his background on the Internet. He had experienced much in his life. He joined the state department two years after finishing law school in 1978. He spent the following twenty-five years in the Middle East taking different high-level and important jobs with the state department and with the embassy. In 1983 he was deputy ambassador during the embassy bombing in Beirut, which resulted in his being injured, suffering a large fragment to his right hip and multiple other serious facial injuries and a broken mandible. Undeterred, he was appointed ambassador to Lebanon and later as ambassador to Jordan. A year ago, he accepted the job as deputy here in Iraq.

However, right now he is just a patient in pain from a kidney stone. A careful history and physical examination was done. He was admitted to the mass casualty ward along with all of his guards and preparations were made for surgery.

The Army infantry is required to carry six ammo clips with twenty rounds in each clip. I immediately noticed that his guards had no less than ten clips and several had twelve or fourteen, plus shock, regular, and smoke grenades. Every member had an M-4 and also a 9-mm on the side. They were all tired and hungry. They were enjoyable to have in the ward and certainly were interesting to watch. Most had been Special Forces, or at least military security police. Most had been at the embassy for a year or two. One was the medic. In the military, a medic acts as their physician, and they all call him "Doc." Oddly enough, when they are around us they seem self-conscious about using the term for their Doc.

Just for fun, I said to their team leader, "I am concerned that you don't have enough fire power, so I will be carrying my 9-mm, just in case you need back up."

I caught him off-guard, and he replied a bit defensively, "There is more than you can see."

"Just joking," I said, "I really just wanted to show you the lay out of the hospital and the cafeteria." Now we were friends.

The Iraqi ward seemed to make him nervous, but not as nervous as the detainee ward, with five detainees and their security police escorts.

"Does everyone know who is here?" he asked.

"Well, this is a hospital and I have never seen a place where information spreads faster, except perhaps in a Mormon church Relief Society women's organization, so I would guess that the answer is yes, almost everyone here would know that the ambassador is here, which is why we put you in your own ward."

Now he was more interested in eating.

Half the team went to eat and the ambassador went to the OR. When we first walked to the ward, the ambassador commented on the dust and dirt on the floor. Then he asked how we kept the ORs clean.

"Well," I started. "You see the ORs are their own separated attachments, not tents like the rest, but specially designed rooms just for surgery. So they are quite different from the rest of the hospital."

I did not mention that the floors were rusted out, and we were all afraid that the bottom would give way due to the weight of the table or the large, heavy C-arm used to do live x-ray while we operated on kidney stones. Nor did I mention that the dips in the floors were so deep that we have to keep moving the tables closer to the edges of the boxes to prevent the floor from caving in. I also purposely did not mention the fact that the joints in the floors leak blood and all other fluids from the patients, making a great place for breeding flies and things no one likes to think about. I did not mention that these leaks were the reason we have fly swatters and fly strips in every corner of the OR. No, the operating rooms are just different from the rest of the tent hospital and located in specially designed rooms just for surgery.

After the security team chief had seen the hospital, I returned to check on the progress of the preparations for going to the OR. The anesthesiologist was at the ambassador's bedside getting ready to walk him back to the OR.

"Has he received the Cipro antibiotic I ordered?" I asked.

"Not yet, but can we just give it to him in the OR?" he asked.

"No, I think it better to be given here," I said. "Of course it will only take a minute so let's hang it here in his IV and I will be right back to get him." He shot an inquisitive look in my direction.

In the hall I explained my comments about the dirt and dust and then asked that the patient be well on his way to anesthesia before he left the room. It was all arranged. I went back to chat. He was comfortable, so I asked him about his daily activities. Apparently he works out, in his own words, "very big deals" between the U.S. government and the most powerful Iraqi sheiks. Of course I really wanted to know exactly what "big deals" meant, but the anesthesiologist had returned. He administered some Versed and Fentanyl to sedate him and we were off to the OR.

Once the ambassador was on the table and just before his airway was intubated, he asked, "What is the one thing that this hospital really needs?"

Suddenly, we were making big deals, and he was still working to win us over. What an opportunity. The hospital has been in dire need of a new CT scanner, but cutting though all of the paper and approval problems had become an enormous barrier.

"Well," I said, "right now there are two major things we need here. First the surgeons need a large, up-armored Ford Excursion to use to get everyone to dinner each night. It is a tradition that we all go together, and now we are riding in the back of an open pick up truck. And the second thing, I guess, would be a new CT scanner for the hospital."

"Good enough," he said as the Propophol anesthesia hit his veins, and he fell into a deep sleep. He was then intubated, the stone identified, laser ablated, large pieces extracted, stent placed, extubated, and on the way to recovery. As expected, in recovery he did not remember making any big deals with me. We would need to find other means to secure transportation for the surgeons to get to dinner, and the colonel still did not have the CT scan problem solved.

After the case I was called back to the secret situation room to talk to someone on General George W. Casey's staff about the ambassador's progress and prognosis. Casey is in charge of the war. As a four-star general, he is the highest ranking officer in the region. He wanted to talk to the ambassador, who was the second highest ranking non-military official in the region.

I explained that this was not a good time, since the ambassador was still asleep. Casey said he would call him when he was awake. That might be an hour I explained, but we could possibly use the satellite phone in the ambassador's room so he did not have to be moved all the way to the command section and have Casey call him there in an hour or two, or he could call Casey from the hospital room directly to his number.

One of the airman in the control center overheard my comment and whispered to me, "The satellite phone is almost out of minutes and will probably cut out in the middle of their conversation."

I covered the receiver while the command surgeon colonel began his own tale of kidney stone adventures.

"Out of minutes?" I asked "Are you serious? This is the U.S. Department of Defense and someone has to put coins in or money in the internet account for the hospital satellite cell phone?"

She shrugged her shoulder and said, "Yes I think so, but Dr. Bishoff, it really is almost empty and will probably cut him off right in the middle of their conversation."

"Sir," I said, "perhaps your assistants can talk to my assistants and get all of the secure numbers so that the ambassador and General Casey can connect this evening."

"Great idea," he replied.

I went to see if the ambassador was awake. Two of his staffers spent about thirty minutes discussing possibilities other than the satellite phone, "which had not been working well," they were told. In the end it was decided that General Casey could just call him in the morning.

I found some food the surgeons had brought back from dinner. The surgeons who are not busy in the OR usually go to dinner together, and bring take-out for the surgeons busy with patients. The usual fare is bar food like burgers, fries, chicken wings, and onion rings. This is one of the rare nice things the surgeons do for each other. Tonight there was a great looking turkey sandwich. After I ate half the sandwich, I went to see the ambassador before going back to bed.

I went over the entire procedure for the third time with him, twice in recovery and now again on the ward. This is not uncommon. I remember my own feelings of complete disgust and indignation when I had my stone treated. Even my own staff members did not have the courtesy to tell me what they found and what they did. My wife reminded me that they had already been by and explained the whole thing three times. Still, I could not remember and wanted to hear about it again.

We went through the entire procedure again. This time he seemed to get it. I asked the same questions as the other two times.

"How much do you remember about our deal?"

"What deal?" he inquired.

Well, that meant no excursion. Unfortunately, he did not hint about any big deals that perhaps we could make. I really should have pursued this before surgery, when we were still dealing with intense kidney pain. Would that have been torture, black mail, secret combination, manipulation or just making very big deals?

Now it was 2200 hours and the ambassador was tired. A sandstorm had shut out the possibility for a helicopter flight to Baghdad so he would be spending the night. He had not slept well for the past three nights. I offered him Ambien, a sleeping aid, and he wanted to take it immediately. The Lieutenant Colonel, nurse turned administrator now caring for the VIP, seemed nervous.

"But General Goerne, the base commander, is coming to see him. What if he is asleep?"

I could not believe what I had just heard. Did she really mean to say that it was more important for the general to see him than for the ambassador to get some rest? We had already been waiting two hours for the general to visit. I was very upset. Was the general her patient or was the ambassador her patient? I almost blurted the question out loud.

I swallowed, smiled, and said, "Since Ambien takes about thirty minutes to work, and since the general is just on his way, we can go ahead and give it to him now so he can get some rest. If he is asleep, the general will certainly understand. He is a very smart man. Anyway, he can always come in the morning, or call like General Casey."

She gave him the Ambien.

Becoming an administrator changes you. I am sure she was a good nurse, but rank and a VIP visit had taken priority over patient care. Oh, please give me a captain or major for a nurse. They really don't care about rank, but they do care about patients. The focus of a nurse administrator, who is usually a lieutenant colonel or a colonel, can seem to be elsewhere at times.

The Levitra product reps have orange and purple pens that fold in half until a small button is pushed, causing the pen to slowly unfold and erect at full length. Since all of the security detail had a good night's sleep and a warm breakfast, I decided to offer a gift from Balad. I told them that I had a new slogan for their squad, "Six clips is barely a good start." They liked it.

One of them said, "Sir, six clips will get you suppressive fire, but if you want to win a battle you will need at least six more to finish the job."

I believed him. I told them they all seemed like stand up guys and anyone with twelve clips needed a pen that could do this. I demonstrated, and as the pen rose to attention, they all burst out laughing. I handed out the pens, making sure each member of the team got one. I glued one of them shut and handed it to the chief of the team and walked away.

As I turned my back to the crowd I heard the chief blurt out, before he could catch himself. "Hey, mine doesn't go up!"

The entire squad burst out laughing.

They called in their helo, and soon the ambassador was on his way back to Baghdad, back to see General Casey and, God willing, to make some really big deals to help win the war, install a new government, write an Iraqi constitution, and send us all home.

60 Minutes Camerman

# Chapter 63

___

# IS *60 MINUTES* REALLY STILL HERE?

5/2/06

My interview with *60 Minutes* was scheduled for later in the afternoon. Their crew of four had set up in OR-I with bright lights in a dark conex box we call the OR one. Monitors were positioned around two camera angles, one in my face and one in Scott Pelley's face. The shots were very tight, and I was sitting uncomfortably close to the interviewer. Normally, I am fairly relaxed, but the idea of the crews and an audience of millions suddenly made me freeze up a little, and I was nervous. My main fear was saying something that could become controversial and make me or the 332nd look bad.

I tried not to dwell on it, but it haunted me. When I had given other interviews on TV, they were about specific topics, like new surgery techniques or public education. This was opened ended, and I did not know what Solly Granatstein was going to feed the interviewer for questions. He had cards with topics for Pelley to ask me, but not the stories themselves. We were finally ready, powder applied to both our faces to take the oily sheen away, last sound check, and then, rolling. One by one he would hand cards to Pelley.

I fielded the usual questions about the war, insurgents and soldiers sharing the hospital and the wards, and my thoughts and experiences in caring for the patients here. Soon I was not nervous and just telling stories. I think they may have gone a bit long, but some things just don't lend themselves to sound bites, certainly these stories didn't. Several stories choked me up a little, and I worried for a few seconds about how that would look on the screen with the tight head shot. But then I noticed that Pelley had tears in his eyes too and on two occasions asked for a break to regain composure.

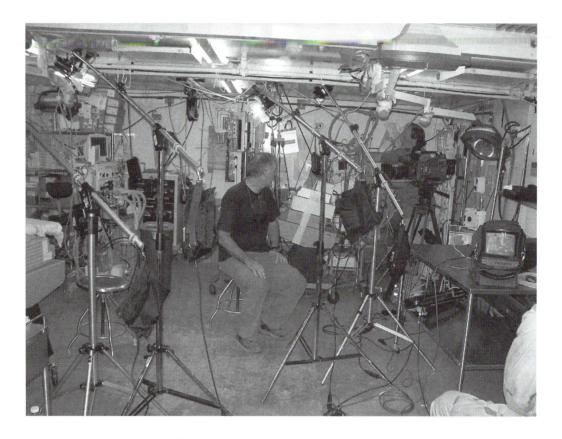

Figure 28. *60 Minutes* sound, lights, and camera set up in operating room #1 just prior to my interview with correspondent Scott Pelley.

My second guessing was interrupted by the realities of my helicopter ride to Abu Ghraib being moved up and the interview running a little late. The techs from the PAD came by to say that the chopper was ten minutes out. I had to change, get my 9-mm, body armor, and equipment to the pad.

Eye Technician

# Chapter 64

---

# THE EYE OF HELL

5/2/06

The chopper picked us up just as the sun was going down, and we were off to the prison in the city of Abu Ghraib, home of infamous stories of torture from Saddam's reign of terror as well as prisoner abuse by our own U.S. forces. Over the past several weeks, I had treated three kidney stone patients from Abu Ghraib. The prisoners were treated in the same manner as we treat U.S. soldiers and with the same equipment: flexible uretoscopy, laser lithotripsy, basket stone extraction, and ureteral stent placement.

Three of the prisoners whom I had previously treated needed their ureteral stents removed. When the detainees come from Abu Ghraib, they arrive on litters by helicopter and with two guards each. For this group that meant six guards and three detainees would have to be flown here, as opposed to me and Sergeant Sechler going there to treat them. I offered to go, and my offer was immediately accepted. Logistically it made sense, so Colonel Taylor agreed. General Goren signed off on the deal as well, and we were now on our way to Abu.

Figure 29. Lt Col Bishoff on make shift stage rarely used at Abu Ghraib.

The flight was only thirty minutes, but in that short time I realized how vulnerable we were. Flying at low altitudes over hostile terrain put us at risk to small-arms fire and rockets capable of taking out our choppers. Our military choppers are loaded with flares, which automatically shoot out if bright lights are detected by the on-board equipment. Flares went off intermittently during the entire flight. We were low enough to see young children running in the streets and men sitting in circles around fires in the courtyards of their homes. Some large homes were on compounds and others merely mud huts. But they were all places from which an insurgent could easily launch a rocket at a passing chopper.

I felt no small amount of relief when we descended into a dusty compound void of trees, grass or even weeds. The site consisted of a camp, and near one end, a large white two-story building with a long central hall and many smaller buildings attached to the side with narrow connecting hallways. As we descended I noticed that the freeway was nearly touching the end of the compound near a grove of palm tress. On the other side were bright lights illuminating the grounds covered with tents, wire, fences, and T barriers.

Sergeant Cook, who was to be our escort, met us at the chopper and helped us load our equipment onto a litter and then into a Humvee. One detainee patient was with us, but he was quickly and separately loaded and transported by ambulance to the hospital.

We drove a short distance to the dusty compound, to an old warehouse building that served as the hospital. Tents were erected inside the hardened facility creating separation of space for privacy and function: one tent for the ER, connected to the OR, another for the wards, and one for the ICU. The rest of the building had been converted to office space, PAD, command section, and weight room. Jail cells were already in place around the area and served as holding areas for the detainees.

Several people came up to greet us, happily asking if we were the 22nd.

"No, we're the 332nd from Balad," we responded each time.

"Oh, we heard that our replacements had arrived. And if that was you, I was going to hug and kiss you!"

It soon became apparent that the happiness and smiles were not for us but for the replacements they hoped were arriving to relieve them so they could go home. After having been in the Abu Ghraib for one year they had earned the chance to be happy and had truly experienced the spectrum offered by opposites in life: light/darkness, pleasure/pain, home/Abu Ghraib.

We soon found out that there is essentially nothing to do at the compound at night except go to the gym or wait for a boxing match scheduled every other Friday night. We were lucky because boxing was tomorrow night. There was no swimming pool, movie theater, popcorn, Burger King, or Pizza Hut. The only option for food was at the dining facility. The Base Exchange was limited in size and supply. Computer access was sparse and limited to work responsibilities, leaving little or no time for personal use to check e-mail or escape from life via the Internet.

After the disappointing introductions (we were still not the 22nd) we were shown to our quarters for the evening. An unused part of the warehouse had been partitioned into a large barracks for hosting Marine units traveling through the area. There were only five small rooms for officers. We were put up in room three, which was secured with a padlock, combination 9544. The room had beds for three—a bunk and single. Sergeant Cook, seemed a bit annoyed when we asked for sheets and blankets. Apparently the Marines carry their own sleeping bags everywhere they go, but we were Air Force! Sheets were secured and at 2100 hours we were off to sleep. At 2400 hours it was time for Marine infantry roll call and a change of patrol. One unit had just returned from patrol in the city, and it took them an hour to settle down, stop laughing, wrestling, shouting, eating, and whacking each other in the testicles. At 0200 there was another roll call and patrol change and again at 0400 hrs and 0600 hrs. I decided trying to sleep or even rest was useless. So I got up, put on my body armor and went to shower and prepare for the day.

Full body armor (U3 posture) including weapons with ammo clips is required twenty-four hours a day everywhere on base except the hospital. One year ago the prison was attacked in a complex and coordinated assault by one hundred armed men and a large vehicle-borne IED. Those at the gates quickly ran low on ammo and it was up to Cobra helicopters to put down the attack. No prisoners were released or harmed. The city is so close that it could happen again, and the attackers could arrive quickly from the surrounding areas in the city. In addition, the compound gets mortared on a regular basis, so it was like being home in Balad. So adding to the misery, dust and unimaginable heat was the need to be in battle gear all day everyday.

On May 5, we pulled the stents and saw an additional six patients, each with different urologic complaints. We performed an additional three cystoscopies to rule out strictures and other problems. I was looking forward to seeing patient 1013, injured from a gunshot wound to the penis and right thigh on March 2. His penis had been ruptured beyond recognition and the reconstruction had gone remarkably well. His follow up was one of the main reasons I wanted to get to Abu Ghraib.

Figure 30. Visiting officers quarters at Abu Ghraib.

After the usual dinner at the dining facility we made our way through rundown and abandoned buildings to the area for fight night. The area was much like an old dairy farm gone broke; all of the buildings were in various stages of decay and badly in need of repair, repairs that would never be made because the farm was dead. In a small courtyard made up of cells-turned-barracks, soldiers had built a small boxing ring out of rope, foam, duct tape, and fence posts for corners. The corner posts were tied down with cargo straps and a come-along to keep the ropes tight. The floor was constructed from the black mats used in the gym to protect the floor. The ring was elevated, built from two-by-six boards. There was a red corner, black corner, bell, referee, score keepers, and wild cigar smoking, cat calling, roof-top and standing-room-only crowd. Any soldier could enter to fight another solider in the same weight category. Grudge fights were also welcome. In fact a grudge match was on the card for that evening. Any two soldiers wishing to settle a score could enter the ring. Each round was three minutes, and each match three rounds, except for the championship matches, which are five rounds.

Figure 31. Official Abu Ghraib Friday night boxing ring.

Tonight, all but one match was a technical knock-out or a real knock-out. Each bout produced bloody noses, which brought a roar from the crowd, already worked to a near frenzy and getting increased energy from each bout. Many fighters were known to the spectators, and most in the crowd had a favorite, but the audience seemed spilt fifty-fifty for each match. No one was spared the cat calls. Despite being young and healthy, three rounds taxed even the youngest athletes.

One match, a grudge match between two soldiers in the same unit, red corner won. After the last mach everyone put on their armor and walked off into the dark of night, back to the cells that once housed Iraqi prisoners. Somehow we were all feeling better after the somewhat brutal event but for reasons hard to explain.

In the morning we were invited by Lieutenant Colonel Mercado, a reservist from New York, to tour the camps with her new replacement, Colonel Hinton. Mercado was a beautiful, rugged woman in her fifties, hardened by life in New York City, but more so from three hundred sixty-five days of living at Abu Ghraib. There was an unmistakable military bearing about her, but at the same time she radiated a deep sense of concern for the medics she commanded and for the prisoners and detainees whose health care was her responsibility.

At the various camps she rattled off detainees numbers as though she were calling out names of long time patients back in New York.

"Where is 187233? He needs to get back to the hospital to see the orthopedic surgeon. How is 183228? His blood sugar levels are running low and he was in hypoglycemic coma last week. It is getting hot. Are you drinking enough water? Let me see that canteen, it better be empty! How about 182266? He never drinks enough; make sure he drinks at least three bottles of water a day." And so it went at each stop.

First we went to Camp Liberty, the site where prisoners go just before being released. About one third of those detained are not guilty of any real crime, usually men in the wrong place at the wrong time. Even though they are guilty of no crime, the average time to freedom for the innocent is eight months. After Liberty, prisoners are moved on to the higher level camps, starting with level five. Level five consists of a small compound guarded by only two guards. Inside the compound are about forty small cell cages, each with a bed, toilet, and blanket. This is where the most dangerous, psychotic or suicidal go. In addition, it is an isolation area for the men with TB, scabies, or leshmaniasis. Most of those cells were full today. Next comes level four, three, two, and finally one.

The mid-level camps consist of a large tent open on all sides in the middle of a piece of land about twenty-by-twenty yards, fenced to a level of about twenty feet and surrounded by wire, with a single-entrance locked gate. There is a water tank for washing that collected the water in the small pond. The pond was drained daily through a PVC pipe leading from the bottom to the fence.

The mid-level camps had about one hundred detainees in each camp. The level one holds up to five hundred detainees under each tent. An occasional volleyball net was seen, but with concertino wire on both the inside and outside surfaces of the fence, volleyball and soccer were treacherous. There was no grass or trees, only dirt, dust, and lots of mud in the rain. There were twelve camps total, all lighted day and night.

All detainees wear yellow jump suits. About fifty new detainees are in-processed each day. At in-processing they lose all their clothing. Then they are searched, showered, finger printed, and retinal scanned. Each has a complete physical, including eye test. Care is delivered for essentially all medical problems. Eye glasses are made and given to those in need. All new detainees go to the hospital for a chest x-ray to rule out TB.

The medics deliver medication twice a day and to those who need it, and even three or four times in the case of several diabetics on insulin. The guards and medics are always in full U-3 body armor. It is usually $120^0$ F in August, rain or shine.

The radio called with a message that I had a meeting with the commander at 1000 hours. Our tour was ending, and so back we went over the two-foot deep hard ruts created during rainy days. The commander was waiting.

Figure 32. Outside view of the hard site prison at Abu Ghraib where Saddam Hussein kept and tortured Iraqi political prisoners.

We had been there for several days and had asked some CIA and base security personnel about the hard site, where the torture under Saddam and abuse by our forces had occurred, but no one wanted to talk about it, let alone show us where it was. That did not stop us from asking. There was a long building essentially covered by tall fences and sitting across the street from the hospital. There did not seem to be any traffic in or out of the area—essentially abandoned. But Sergeant Sechler and I commented on the strange darkness that seemed to be present when we walked past it.

The commander thanked us for venturing to Abu Ghraib to see prisoners and save a lot of travel by his already thin staff. Then he mentioned that CIA had reported to him that we had been asking around base about the hard site and then he asked if we wanted a private tour and pointed, across the street from the hospital to the building that had emitted darkness and evil.

Under Saddam Hussein's regime, the most dangerous physical and political prisoners were held in the hard site. Many books and articles have been written about this prison. There were approximately thirty thousand men housed in twelve-by-twelve-foot cells holding up to forty men each. Here Saddam would torture his enemies and hold weekly hangings. A gas chamber was near the death house. In 1984 Saddam responded to prisoner complaints of overcrowding by ordering three thousand to the upper level, and then ordered his son to shoot every third prisoner in the head. The other two thousand were used to carry out the dead, one for the arms and one for the legs. The bodies were dumped in a large mass grave near the hard site and covered with dirt. This area was the only green, thriving spot with large trees. Political prisoners were tortured in several rooms at the top of the longest mile or hung from the dual metal gallows.

Figure 33. Upper level of Abu Ghraib prison where it was reported that Saddam Hussein ordered 1000 men shot in response to prisoners complaints of overcrowding.

After the 2003 invasion of Iraq, Saddam's prisoners were freed and the building emptied. The United States turned the hard site and the Abu Ghraib prison into a center for processing detainees. This is when the famous detainee abuse scandal occurred. Once the photos of U.S. guards torturing and degrading Iraqi prisoners hit the press, the site was closed and other cells in the prison were utilized to hold them. The hard site prison was then given back to the Iraqi government to use as a prison once again. In 2006, the six Iraqi physicians working at the prison were killed by insurgents, and the Iraqi government tried to get the U.S. military to take care of their political prisoners. Eventually the military forced the Iraqis to move their prisoners to another site. Workers were hired to clean the prison, but after three weeks of accomplishing nothing, the Iraqis workers were fired and the doors locked leaving the place essentially frozen in time.

Figure 34. Gallows at Abu Ghraib used by Saddam Hussein's government for weekly executions of political prisoners, similar to the one used by the Iraqi government to execute Hussein on 30 December 2006.

We went back to the clinic to see more patients, including patient 1013. I initially thought I would have to amputate his penis, but after he was cleaned up and carefully examined I felt there was enough tissue for reconstruction. He was led into the exam room with blind folds and put on the exam table. Through the interpreter, I asked if I could see his injury. He started shaking and asked why. When the interpreter told him the surgeon who repaired the injury was here to check up on him, he tried to leap off the tablet to hug and thank me, but before this could be translated, the two guards slammed him back to the table.

He was surprised and happy to see me. He had looked at the injury and wondered if he would lose his parts or bleed to death from the rapid oozing at the site of impact. After the surgery, he recovered quickly. He was urinating without problems and even having partial erections.

We tried to see patient 1037, who was engaged by our Special Forces and shot in the left thigh and scrotum with injury to his testicles as well. They found his records, but because the records detailing his arrest were never sent to Abu Ghraib, despite being requested, he was held for thirty days (which is about the time it took to heal his wounds) and then released.

After dinner we went back to the hospital to wait for our chopper back to Balad. We had not done much, but we were exhausted. Being wakened every two hours by the Marines in the adjacent barracks, the heat, and the conditions in general had worn me out in just two days. These soldiers were there for a year.

After a hard year at the prison, their replacements were arriving, and in a week they would be going home. Most of the staff had gone to camp Mohammed for a big party. Only a tech, nurse, and one doctor were in the ER. A call came over the radio that four Marines were critically injured and on the way to the hospital. The ER doc asked if I would stay and help while the others, their party interrupted, made the mile walk from the housing area back to the hospital. Minutes later the doors opened and in ran two Marines frantically pushing a litter through the ER, bumping into tables and trays along the way. The ER nurse told them to slow down, but they were undeterred, a comrade's life was at stake. The Marine on the litter was badly injured, his life forever changed after his Humvee ran over an IED planted in the road that he and his squad were patrolling in order to prevent IED and other acts of terrorism.

Now his buddies were running full speed ahead, but with no idea where to go or stop until the ER doctor yelled, "Stop! Put him right here."

I was totally taken back by the look of terror on the faces of the marines. As I glanced at the patient I experienced the same initial shock they had been wrestling with for the past twenty minutes since the IED explosion.

On the NATO litter was the trunk of a young man, now missing both legs above the knees. Dirt and grim covered the rest of his abnormally angulated arms, and his mutilated face and head. It was a combination of smoke, dirt, mud, blood, and bone that covered him from his stumps to his head. Under the grime I could see a severely disfigured face with teeth showing in places you don't normally see teeth. He had a mangled left arm that had little normal feeling when I grabbed it to move him to the stretcher. He also felt very cold to touch. I realized that his breathing tube was not attached to a bag, but a nurse appeared with a bag and began respiration. A surgeon walked in and started to help the ER doc with the code. The techs started removing his clothing and one started chest compressions.

The patient's unit medic was trying to give someone a report, and no one was listening. They knew their jobs, but he wanted desperately to tell us, the Marine's hospital team, what had happened. I was not immediately needed while they undressed him and started CPR, so I turned to listen to the medic. He had large tears streaming down his very dirty face. His hands were still in gloves covered with blood, as were his clothes.

"The lead hummer hit an IED," he began, "I tried to intubate him in the field, but after a few minutes realized that the tube was in his esophagus. I think I killed him, Doc. I tubed the esophagus. We put tourniquets on both legs and his arm. His face was all messed up, his jaw broken and his lips partially blown off. His left arm is broken in at least three places. I could not get an IV, and I am sorry, but I put the tube in his esophagus."

The tears got larger. I put my arm around his shoulder and pulled him very close to me so that he could hear despite the noise in the room and said,

"He is lucky to have a medic like you. You did everything you could do, and you did everything just right. Everyone puts a tube in the esophagus now and then, but you recognized it and replaced it. You did everything just the way we wanted it done."

He finally looked up at me and nodded and sobbed.

"They need some help with lines," I said. I left him and went to help.

What they really needed was some help opening the chest. I moved up to help the surgeon who decided to crack the chest as one last ditch effort and possibly one chance to show the other Marines that we would go all out for them. Sechler held my Luminex flash light over the field while we made the incision, then used the large knife and mallet to open the sternum. I held the chest open because we could not find the rib spreader. The surgeon placed a clamp on his aorta. The Marine's heart was not beating in an organized fashion, but quivering. The heart seemed to be empty. Once the clamp was in place I inserted a line in his subclavian vein and more blood was given. The surgeon continued open heart massage while lidocaine, epinephrine, bicarbonate, and more blood and fluid given. His pH returned at 6.9 and his hematocrit 12 percent. A normal hematocrit for this young man would be approximately 40 percent. He had lost almost all of the blood volume in his body from his injuries. His heart stopped beating. His heart and skin were cold. He could not survive the massive total body trauma.

The kind of blast that can tear the legs off a young strong man in less than a second caused this injury. That is what killed the Marine, not an initially misplaced ET tube. I turned to see the unit medic staring at a dead member of his squad. Somehow I felt he was looking beyond dead, dirty, mangled buddies, seeing soldiers in happier times, trying to smack each other on the testicles, or cheering at Friday night fights, or some other good memory of life. Behind his blank stare were tears and a look of desperation, lacking any sign of hope. I grabbed him and pulled him close to me again and told him the very same thing that I knew, that he had done everything he could. I wanted him to know I believed it from the very core of my being. I needed him to understand that he did not kill the member of his squad. Somehow later this week, possibly even tomorrow, this stunned medic would be back in the streets of Abu Ghraib on patrol with the rest of his squad. A glimmer of relief in his eyes told me that he believed me.

A tech from the helicopter pad grabbed my arm and said, "Dr. Bishoff, your chopper is landing on the pad right now. If you are going to leave tonight, you need to leave now."

The surgeon asked for the time. 2143 hours, and then he called a stop to the code. Another Marine was dead, but not because of his team medic.

As I walked to the hall to don my body armor, I realized there was something cold on my left leg. There was a large blood-stain on my thigh; it was from the patient's left leg stump, which had been against my leg while I inserted a femoral line.

We flew to Biop for fuel, then to Baghdad 10th Tenth CSH to pick up a patient, and finally back to Balad. During the flight the rushing air in the helo cabin caused the wet blood stain to feel colder and colder, reminding me of the arms and limbs of the precious owner of the life giving substance. I reviewed and replayed the scene over and over in my mind and could not get the image of the medic out of my mind. I could clearly see his twenty-year-old boyish face with the look of terror in his eyes, tears streaming down his cheeks, repeating, "I think I killed him, Doc."

Flares on the chopper were being shot out about every ten minutes on the way back to base. When we finally arrived inside the wire, I felt a great sense of relief. A safety-of-home feeling came over me. I was suddenly very tired.

Radiology Technician

# Chapter 65

_____

# SMOKING AND KIDS WITH RPG

5/14/06

Having been away from the base for several days, I returned to a very busy clinic. There is no way to let people know I am away before they arrive. No secretaries to schedule your visits and call them at their tent cities to let them know I will be in Abu Ghraib for a the weekend, so we hang a sign on the door that says "the Urology clinic will be closed until approximately 14 May 2006. In an average day I will see six patients, but today twelve were waiting.

Almost everyone in the Army smokes or at least it seems that way. The tobacco companies' biggest fear in the 1960s was that if we all knew how bad cigarettes were for us, we would stop smoking, and they would lose money. They may even have to sell some of their ten million dollar homes and recreation properties and be forced to get respectable jobs. But as is often the case in life, the companies' fears turned out to be baseless; people now know tobacco is terrible for their health, but they smoke anyway.

Here, if a patient does not smoke, I look at them and ask, "Are you telling me that you are in the Army and you don't smoke cigarettes?" Suddenly they look scared.

Their response is predictable. "Yes, sir, that's right I don't smoke."

Then I usually say, "Soldier, does your first sergeant know about this?"

Catching the joke, they laugh.

On the other hand, if they smoke I usually say, "Let me see. Smoking stinks, is expensive, and is guaranteed to kill you. Help me understand why you do that."

Normally they say they know it is bad for their health and are trying to stop. Or they tell me how many times they have tried to quit but are unable.

Sometimes they say they are going to stop when they go home, "Cause my wife don't allow smoking in the house or around the kids."

The fact is they probably won't stop, and for almost 60 percent of them, they won't have a wife when they get home from this war, and that will be one more reason for them to keep on smoking. The tobacco companies win again, at least for now.

When I have a patient who tells me that his wife is leaving or has left him, I ask what he plans to do when he goes home.

Without exception the answer is, "Well, since I don't have a wife anymore, and I need to support my kids, I re-enlisted."

Publicly the Army says it is creating programs to help and I am certain they are. On the other hand they now have a re-enlisted soldier who does not have a wife when he deploys again next year.

So today I started espousing the evils of tobacco by telling a nineteen-year-old infantry soldier stationed in a very dangerous city, Ramadi. Tobacco will cause cancer, heart attacks, strokes, and, of course, erection problems.

He looked me in the eye. With profound seriousness and a bit of fear he said, "I am just not looking that far into the future right now, sir. I am trying to survive day to day."

I believed him.

Toward the end of the day things slowed a bit, and I realized I had rushed through some of the patients. I asked a young first lieutenant about the wildest thing he had seen in Iraq.

He told a story of being on patrol and catching a glimpse of something metal protruding from a second story window. He looked with his binoculars and to his surprise saw a young boy aiming a rocket propelled grenade at their convoy. The boy was small and appeared to be struggling to maneuver the rocket. He stumbled and fell back from the open window. Seconds later, he reappeared with the rocket, apparently standing on a chair or stool. The lieutenant could see that he had stabilized himself and was taking aim in their direction. The lieutenant immediately directed fire from his squad into the window, destroying the window, a large part of the front of the house, as well as the child and most of his family.

"I did not have a choice really" the lieutenant said.

"No, you didn't," I said, "but it must be hard at times to think about the whole incident."

"All the time," he replied.

General Surgeon

# Chapter 66

_____

# 'NURSE, NURSE ... AM I THE WORST BURNED?'

5/15/06

Burns are devastating and represent the worst possible injury a human can suffer. They are the ultimate trauma research model, and we certainly witnessed a lot of burn patients in Iraq. During our rotation, several tent fires caused permanent changes in the lives of some of our soldiers. One tent fire resulted from an unattended cooking stove and another from a small propane warmer used by several soldiers as they slept on a cold morning following an all night patrol.

I once watched a short but illustrative video of a modular large GP tent made of the same material as our tent hospital and clinic. It was set afire and within seconds the entire tent was engulfed in flames. The video and the burn patients from tent fires prompted me to carry a large knife in my right BDU pocket so that I could cut my way straight through the wall of any tent the very second I had the inclination that it was on fire. Fortunately, I never had to use the knife.

Nevertheless, burns plagued our rotation. The following burn story has a powerful, compelling message about the dedication and devotion of our military leaders. The incident did not occur during our rotation but happened during the rotation preceding ours. The story was fresh on the minds of the medics we replaced, and I had heard it from several people who were in the hospital when it happened. They cared for the burn patients that day and retold the story to those of us just arriving. I also confirmed the story with Colonel Steven Lynch, the urologist at Balad whom I replaced and was there when it happened. This is a story that must be told.

The infantry use the Bradley fighting vehicles in many areas of Iraq to transport troops with armor protection while providing covering fire to suppress enemy troops. The Bradley typically holds a crew of three in the front: a commander, a gunner, and a driver in the front; and there are six fully equipped soldiers in the rear compartment.

Usually the senior squad leader or platoon sergeant has a seat in the rear closest to the door. When the door goes down the leaders are the first out to lay down suppressive gun fire, and the more junior infantry follow their leaders, who are leading from the front by example with courage and confidence. One weakness with some of the Bradley models is that the fuel tank is in the center of the vehicle, and if it is struck by a rocket propelled grenade an explosive fire ball consumes fuel, ignites ammunition, starts the metal on fire, and, of course, destroys the human personnel inside.

On this particular day, one Bradley was in fact strategically and tragically struck in the center with a rocket propelled grenade igniting the fuel tank, metal frame, and ammo in the vehicle. Three crew and six troops were in the vehicle when it was attacked. The forward crew quickly died from the impact. Smoke and fire immediately filled the troop compartment. The rear door was released by the platoon sergeant in the rear seat so they could evacuate. Initially the events of the day were not clear to the ER personnel caring for severely burned infantry soldiers and the precise details will likely never be known, but they are not essential to appreciate the rest of the story.

When burned soldiers were coming, the ER activated the mass casualty pager, and nurses, ER personnel, and surgeons descended to help. It had already been a busy several days, and the staff was emotionally and physically worn. But American soldier burn patients filled the tent and were getting the care they deserved.

One of the men with severe third degree burns had little left of his uniform; the fire had burned off his cloths and melted the soles of his boots. His skin was peeling from nearly every surface, his hair completely gone, and his face was rapidly swelling and beyond recognition. He kept asking his nurse if he was the worst burned. At first she did not pay much attention to his inquiry but instead continued to do all she needed to do with the appropriate sense of urgency. He kept asking the same question, "Am I the worst burned?" This soldier needed to be intubated and resuscitated and sent to the OR for long incisions to be made on his arms and legs through the skin into the dense covering of the muscles to allow the tissue to swell without stopping blood flow to his extremities and then, if he lived, air evacuated to Germany and then to the States. So the nurse did not have much time or patience trying to decide if one was worse than the other and did not see why it could possibly matter, so she ignored the question and worked to save his life. The normally compassionate and patient nurse was simple exhausted.

When he asked the question gain, she looked at him and said with a hint of impatience in her voice, "Look, everyone in here is severely burned!"

The soldier reached out with his severely burned hand to touch her arm and said, "I am the platoon sergeant. These are my boys, and if I am not the worst burned then I have failed my men."

Suddenly she understood that it did indeed matter. In tears she looked into the eyes of a dying platoon sergeant, who knew more about duty, responsibility, and leadership than the rest of us will ever know, and said, "Yes, you are the worst burned."

The answer seemed to give immediate relief, and he relaxed, closed his eyes and responded by saying something like "Then today is a great day. I did my duty."

Later in the day the staff would get more of the story from the other troops in the same convoy with the destroyed Bradley. Apparently once the rear compartment door was opened and the two senior leaders rolled out into fresh air, the platoon sergeant went back into the inferno, rushing head first into the flame-and smoke-filled troop compartment while he held his breath to retrieve one of his men, who had been severely burned and overcome with smoke. Then he went back through the flames again and again until all of his boys were out of the vehicle. The platoon sergeant would later die of his wounds, and he would die with peace of mind simply because he did his duty and he was the worst burned!

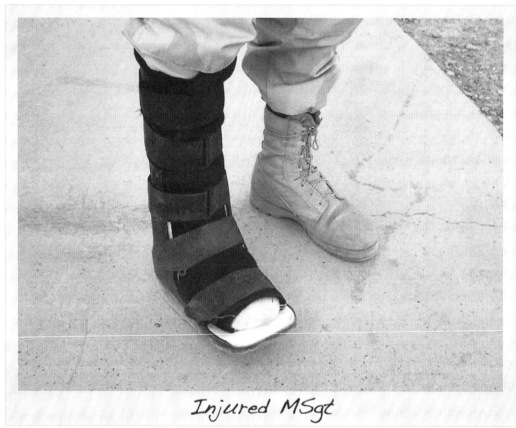

Injured MSgt

# Chapter 67

_____

# HOUSE CALL TO THE EMBASSY

5/16/06

Several weeks ago we performed a kidney stone removal on the second highest-ranking U.S. political figure in Iraq. He worked closely with the Iraqi government to draft their new constitution and has made many other important contributions to the new government.

Now it was time to have his stent removed. One option was to have him fly here with his twelve man security team for a five minute procedure. Another option was to send the equipment to Baghdad and have the urologist there, who had referred him in the first place, pull the stent. Another option was for me to volunteer to fly to Baghdad and do the procedure. I was nervous about flying to Baghdad because of recent instances of choppers being shot down, so I sent three sets of disposable graspers to the urologist there to use to pull the stent.

The procedure was scheduled for May 14, and while we normally do this in the clinic the urologist had lined up the OR to administer some IV sedation. Two days before the scheduled procedure, the urologist called to say that his scope was non-functional, and he would need loaner equipment. Our scope was also broken and for the past month we had been using a flexible bronchoscope to do cystoscopy to remove stents, but not without some difficulty. The bronchoscope is almost nine inches longer that the cystoscope, and so the usual stent graspers are not long enough to pass through to the end of the scope. Instead of stent graspers we had been using kidney stone baskets, which are long enough to stick out the end of the scope. However, they require the operator to find the open (free end of the bladder coil), get the end inside the open basket, and maneuver the basket far enough down the stent to hold it during extraction. This unorthodox procedure is challenging for the urologist and, as a result, fun to do. Sending our bronchoscope to them was out of the question, and our ICU docs were not excited about me taking the bronchoscope to the city for more that a short period of time, since they also use it on a regular basis to treat problems in the ICU.

The regular military chopper schedule would require me to fly out on Saturday night at midnight and then return Sunday night at midnight. I did not really want to be in the city that long, so I explained the situation to the ambassador's secretary at the embassy. While I waited on the phone he solved the problem by sending our own chopper to pick us up at 0800 Sunday morning. At

0805 the chopper sound could be heard coming from the direction of Baghdad, and seconds later two birds were on the pad at the hospital. One of the load masters motioned for us, and we boarded the one in the first position. Once our gear was secured and our seat belts fastened, we lifted off and headed back to the city. The morning was spectacular, clear sunny skies with cool temperatures and low winds. They gave me a set of head phones, I exchanged greetings with the pilot and off we went. They offered to bring us back an hour earlier, if we wanted, since they had a scheduled mission at that time, or they would bring us back at 1400 as previously scheduled. We flew over the farm lands of Balad and the mud-hut homes of the local Iraqis.

Figure 35. Former amusement park for high ranking officials in the Saddam Hussein government Ba'ath Party.

As we approached the city the homes improved, but junk piles remained a constant at every home regardless of the occupant's economic status. Soon we were inside the city with the crowded streets, apartments, and buildings. The city was beautiful. Large colorful domed mosques dotted the skyline. The famous hotels bombed during the raids were right before my eyes, in real life. There was the military stadium with crossed swords, the tomb of the unknown, and the destroyed Ba'ath government headquarters and, of course, the palaces.

When we arrived at the Washington Pad near the embassy, we were greeted by state department security guards who escorted us to their up-armored Suburban. The doors were very heavy and later I learned that they weigh four hundred pounds each. The protective glass is several inches thick. The interior was pretty much the same as ours, but the ride was stiffer. At the 10th CSH we were immediately escorted to the back of the hospital and then to a waiting area where the hospital commander was sitting with the patient telling him about his own urology adventures. We all chatted while Sergeant Sechler set up the equipment.

The patient was taken to the OR and after a small amount of IV sedation, the stent was removed in a total time of 60 seconds. While we chatted outside the OR with the patient's personal security guard, we were informed that he was awake. The guard mistakenly left and went to the recovery room to wait for us. About the time he left two Iraqi nationals with badges stuffed in their front shirt pockets so that it was impossible to see them walked up to the OR doors and into the patient's room. I stopped them coming in the door and asked them who they were. They were in civilian cloths, not scrubs, and did not speak English. I scanned the hall for the security team and none of them were on the floor—a big screw up. I asked if any of the OR staff knew the Iraqi nationals and none did.

Finally one of them pulled out his badge indicating he was from the cleaning crew and we sent them away.

The ambassador was loaded into the elevator, which descended to the lower level for recovery, where the entire team, including the personal guard, was waiting. I was surprised to see so many nationals in the hospital working at odd jobs. None were being guarded like the third country nationals in Balad.

While the patient recovered from the sedation, the 10th CSH urologist showed us around the hospital. It had been the royal family's hospital during Saddam's rule. It was a great facility, reminding me of an older community hospital, aging but stable. I was impressed with the high ceilings and solid floors, which I had missed during the four months at Balad working in tents and conex box operating rooms with rusted out floors. The surgeons had nice hotel-style rooms in the hospital complex. There were a lot of swimming pools formerly owned by Saddam's sons, now used by hundreds of servicemen and state department staff.

Once our patient was awake, we rode with him in his limo back to the embassy compound, which was Saddam's former palace. Inside we ate lunch in one of the ornate and detailed waiting rooms. All of the ceilings were covered with plastic cutouts hand painted in beautiful colors. In the ballroom a large painted mural of scud missiles was carefully painted and still preserved on the wall. Many of the door frames were broken down at the time of the initial invasion.

Figure 36. Outside one of many palaces turned into office space for U.S. and Coalition forces.

The outside looked exactly how it appeared on TV during the invasion. After lunch, pictures, and a tour, it was time to return to Balad. The state department security guard, Ed Fairchild, told us about his days as a Navy SEAL and some of his encounters with Rice, Clinton, Bush, Rumsfeld, and Powell as we walked several blocks to the helicopter landing called Washington PAD. At 1305 hours the two Black Hawks landed and waved us aboard. We lifted off and headed back to Balad with lots of memories and a camera full of photos. In just several weeks we had seen the extremes of the country, from the worst in Abu Ghraib to the finest in Baghdad and the presidential palace.

Figure 37. View from helicopter of downtown Baghdad, Iraq.

Once again we passed over the new construction of the city, the crossed swords parade grounds, empty school yards, amusement parks, and a miniature golf area, all abandoned and in poor repair. We flew over the palace, congested apartments, and street markets and out to the edge of the city with the mud huts and farm lands. Eventually we once again had the good feeling of seeing the gunners put down their machine guns as we passed over the welcome site—miles of T-barriers surrounding the perimeter of Balad air base.

C-17 Crew Chief

# Chapter 68

---

# DAILY ROUTINE

5/19/06

Only one new story this week. We are trying to remain focused on the mission, but 80 percent of the hospital staff have been replaced by the new incoming team and have returned to the United States or are waiting for flights. The planes are constantly "broken" leading to large backups and delays. Twenty people from our rotation are still here in Balad three days after their scheduled departure date. Last night, they were actually loaded on the bus and driving to the plane when they were delayed for thirty minutes at the flight line entry control point. They had to return to the passenger terminal with a "no go" for the night. It is an emotional roller coaster. Our replacements are one day late in arriving. It is hard to remain centered and to not think about postponing cases or putting off work needing to be done.

I admitted two new stone patients and was in the ER all morning with an unusual case. A patient with severe bleeding from the urinary system was losing about a half unit of blood every hour. We obtained a CT scan but could not determine the ultimate source of the bleeding. We sent her to Germany for angiography and further work up. I called them to let them know about her arrival, and as has been the case the entire four months, they were not very interested in her case. They were, however, quick to point out the appropriate management course, which is not available here in Iraq at our facility or any facility in Iraq. If I had my way I would make their urologists come here and spend a month so they can see what we are doing and finally understand our mission.

I inquired about a patient sent to them eight days ago. He was seen on a routine basis in the clinic and today is Friday, so they scheduled him for surgery on Monday. They lack a sense of urgency and care for these patients. My goal on a daily basis is not to send any one to Germany! Occasionally I fail and have to turn the patient over to their care.

I continue to ask patients about the wildest thing they have seen in Iraq. The responses are similar: IEDs, small arms attacks, RPG attacks. I understand that these are significant and wild events, but it's the same story with almost every soldier. To record the same thing would not be interesting for the reader, but do be aware of how significant living through even one IED can be to the nineteen or twenty year old who joined the service to better his or her life and get ahead in the world. I have not met a soldier who has not lost at least one member of their unit to an attack or an IED. They almost expect it to happen or to be injured during their time here. Nevertheless, they get up, suit up, patrol, drive convoys, fly choppers and simply do the job the United States of America has asked them to do.

Today I asked about wild events and a very steady twenty-year-old infantry soldier told me about the awe he experienced as he watched a dense sand storm engulf their post in Ramadi. He described the scene as it unfolded from his vantage point on a building. The leading edge of the storm moved slowly across the base until even the lights were obscured. The sun beat down through the dense sand casting a dark Halloween orange glow and eerie dark brown hue to the sky and surrounding buildings. You have the feeling of being smothered and, in fact, there are cases this year of deaths after being trapped out in the open during a dense sand storm.

"It was just like in the movies, but real. It was by far the wildest thing I have ever seen in my life. Even more wild than a few IED blasts."

Another patient today was a truck driver. He drives almost everything but usually the five-ton tractor-trailer eighteen-wheeler rig, all up-armored and *Star Wars* looking. He has been trying to hit stray dogs with the rig every chance he gets to "rid the country of the scavengers." Last week as they were approaching an Iraqi military checkpoint, he spotted a large dog lying in the road just about twenty yards from the check point. He did not slow down and saw his dream of crushing the dog coming true. Suddenly the dog jumped up but was standing on two legs running for his body armor. One of the Iraqi guards had become tired and for reasons known only to the Iraqi guard had chosen to take a nap in front of the check point. That nap got him introduced to the screeching tires of a five-ton.

"Just when I think I have seen it all, they surprise me again and again," he said.

C-130 Crew Chief

# Chapter 69

———

# TAGGED OUT

5/20/06

Finally, our replacements have arrived. We picked them up at the H-6 housing and took them and some of the other surgeons back to their rooms and to the hospital. After breakfast and a nap we would orient them to their jobs and to the hospital. The new surgeons, techs and anesthesia crew all had a strong attitude of arrogance, which would hurt them later in the evening. All of them, I'm sure, are competent to do their jobs under normal circumstances. The differences here are the sheer mechanics, equipment, and nuances of being in combat and working at a combat hospital. The lab and pharmacy personnel exhibited the same inappropriate attitude and ignored too many teaching points. Later in the evening they would realize how big of a mistake this would be. With few exceptions, the old staff was frustrated by the lack of attention from the new staff about the lessons they had learned under fire. The new personnel did not hear our pleas and instruction. Arrogance had blinded their eyes and shut their ears.

The morning and early afternoon was quiet for a Sunday, which was normally one of the busiest days of the week. That made us nervous, but only added to the newcomers' feelings of adequacy. The new anesthesia group was informed that because of their late arrival they would only have one day to see the equipment and to talk to the outgoing staff. They chose to go back and sleep after lunch. The outgoing staff reminded them that they would be leaving at 1700 hours for the PAX terminal to catch their home-bound flight. They acknowledged the fact and chose to go off to sleep.

The new trauma chief sent e-mails months earlier informing every one of his great capabilities as a surgeon and manager and that there was no one better suited for the job of trauma director. He also ignored the wisdom of the outgoing director, Lieutenant Colonel Jeff Bailey, and encouraged his early departure on Sunday afternoon. Bailey had been scheduled to give the entire new surgery staff a briefing on how to manage a mass-casualty situation and the overall rules of engagement between the services, but the new trainer wanted to give it instead and promised to do it in the afternoon after Bailey had left. He decided to let the surgeons go back to sleep, canceled the briefing, and rescheduled it for later in the week. By early Sunday afternoon, the lab, pharmacy, ER, anesthesia, and surgery staffs had given as much of an orientation as their replacements would allow so they departed to the PAX terminal to catch a flight home. None felt comfortable, but off they went.

At 1800 hours the call came to the ED that twelve soldiers had been injured in an IED blast and all were on the way to the 332nd. Twenty minutes later they arrived and were being treated. Luckily, many were just walking wounded with through and through injures, minor bleeding, no head or severe extremity injuries. Another call came: eight injured by a complex vehicle-borne IED followed by a wall of small-arms fire. It was followed by a call for ten more. Soon there were four choppers on the pad and five hovering in the air waiting to unload. Now there were thirty patients in an ER built to hold fourteen.

Despite all of the people in the ER there was absolute chaos at every level. No one was in charge. Where was the trauma director? The staff nurse did not know about the situation in the ER. No one had activated the mass-casualty pager system. There were few surgeons around, most had gone back to sleep. The lab was telling the ER it would take sixty minutes to get blood for the dying patients. Earlier in the day, with experienced staff, it would have taken ten minutes. Who was next for CT? Who was going to the OR? I found the trauma director and asked him how I could help him. Whenever I asked Bailey, our trauma director, that question, I was quickly assigned several patients to triage, X-ray, define injuries, fill out buck slips for the OR and then filter back to him to get the lineup for the OR. He kept a list base on our detail assessment and made the call about priority. He was a great trauma coordinator.

The new trauma chief lied and said he had it under control and that I was not needed. There was a gunshot wound to the back, no bladder catheter and hypotensive.

My new replacement seemed overwhelmed at the sight. I paused for a minute to see if any were going immediately to the OR, so I could help if needed, since there were no surgeons around. But the new trauma chief again indicated that they were in good shape.

"Who is next for CT?" the radiology tech yelled for the third time.

No one responded. I took Eric Hick, Sechler, and the new replacement tech out of the ER and back to the clinic so they could catch their breath. It was going to get busy.

About forty-five minutes later we returned to the ER and almost nothing had changed. The beds had the same patients in them; the gunshot wound to the back was now getting blood but had not been scanned. Lieutenant Colonel Jay Johannigman was one of the new staff surgeons and had been one of my staff at Wilford Hall during residency. He suddenly appeared, just from a nap. Angry about not having been awakened, he began to take charge. He immediately ordered the gunshot wound back to the OR.

"He does not have any films," insisted the new trauma director.

Johannigman indicated he did not need them because if the bleeding was not stopped, he would die. So to the OR. He now had a bladder catheter in place full of dark red blood, so we changed into scrubs and went to OR-I. I grabbed a head light, knowing that the newcomers would not know that the overhead lights in the conex box ORs were not useful. Exploratory laparotomy showed a bullet entrance from the front of the abdomen with a large exit wound in the left flank resulting in a ruptured spleen, a shattered kidney with active bleeding from the kidney blood vessels, and a large hole in the diaphragm.

The general surgeons removed the spleen, and then I moved them over so Eric Hick and I could take out the kidney. The general surgeon bristled at the thought that he was not capable of the procedure. But we immediately moved him from his spot, and we moved in for a quick nephrectomy. In anticipation of this scenario I had brought a vascular stapler. The kidney was hard to see; the bleeding was not. I pushed Hick to work faster to free up the kidney with blunt dissection using his hands and laparoscopic knowledge of the anatomy. With some help the kidney was soon held only by its artery and vein. Two passes with the stapler and the kidney was in the bucket and the bleeding stopped. We lingered to check out the diaphragm and the retroperitoneum to be sure our site was not bleeding. It was not, so we scrubbed out.

Back in the ER patients were slowly being moved out. Colonel Taylor, our commander, had not been replaced and he had just pulled the trauma director from a room where he was scrubbed and forced him back to the ER to finish the triage and assignments. There was a terse exchange that caused a frown to appear on the commander's face and the veins to pop out from his forehead. He had the last word and the trauma director went off to the ER.

We walked past the mass-casualty ward, normally ready for mass casualty and commonly empty, but now full. Fifteen patients from the wounded-but-walking group were there having to wait for films and washout of their wounds. All were Kurds. They all kept silent but were tracking each doctor entering the room, hoping it would be their turn next. The Kurds are a different people to be sure. Fifteen Iraqis would have all been yelling, calling for pain medication and screaming for the doctor's attention, no matter how minor the wound. Not the Kurds. Eric Hick seemed to have had enough. The look on his face made me realize that it was time to get him back to bed. I would be leaving the next day. I had his attention. Tomorrow would be the most productive day for our overlap.

Surgical ICU Director

# Chapter 70

——

# ETHICAL DILEMMAS OF WAR SURGERY, *USA TODAY* STORY

Gregg Zoroya and his cameraman were sent from *USA Today* to do stories about the war. They were different from most of the others who came seeking stories for their sponsors. We hosted may visiting journalists, but for the most part they seemed more like tourists. They rarely seemed genuinely interested in finding out what was happening in the hospital. They would do some cursory interview, take a bunch of pictures of the tent hospital and off they went. Many came with an agenda or preconceived notion about the war and looked carefully for pieces to fit what they had already scripted in their minds.

Zoroya and his cameraman were different. They did not visit for a few hours, but stayed for days if not weeks, just to get one or two stories. They literally did embed themselves with the troops and battled to win our confidence so that they could actually get a glimpse into the reality of war. They went out on evacuation missions where soldiers were being recovered and where live fire was encountered. While they shot pictures U.S. soldiers returned fire to secure the landing zone. They accompanied soldiers back to the hospital, to surgery, to the ward and to air evac in order to see the entire process, not just a tiny snap shot in time, but the entire time line. As a result I developed a great sense of respect for them as true professionals.

When traveling I always pick up a copy of *USA Today* and look for a Zoroya story, because if one is there, it's going to be honest reporting. Zoroya wrote a brilliant piece that captures ethical dilemmas of this and any war and how the surgeons dealt with those daily challenges.

**Wartime adds dimensions to dilemmas doctors face**
By Gregg Zoroya, USA TODAY 5 June 2006
(Reprinted with Permission)

Bagdad, Iraq - After a helicopter rushed Army Spc. Ethan Biggers to the military hospital here in March, neurosurgeons left the operating room shaken by the extensive damage to his brain. A sniper had shot Biggers, 21, through the head, and the wound looked as bad as any that doctors Brett Schlifka and Hans Bakken had seen.

"If he came into my hospital in the States, gunshot wound to the head, eyes fixed and dilated, not a chance I would take him into the O.R. Not a chance," says Schlifka, 35, of Philadelphia. "(We'd) tell his family it's a non-survivable injury."

But Schlifka and Bakken, both Army majors, had long before made a pact something they would not have done back home. Because counseling a family in a war zone is impossible, and because the U.S. military offers no guidelines on whether to withhold treatment for severely brain-damaged casualties, the doctors had decided to err on the side of life. No matter how severe the brain injury, no matter how hopeless the case, they vowed to keep a soldier alive long enough to get him out of the war zone, if only so his family could see him one last time.

For Schlifka, Bakken, 37, and other doctors at one of the busiest battlefield hospitals in Iraq, the war has created new or more complicated moral and ethical dilemmas. Here, doctors often face profound personal choices treating the most disturbing wounds they have seen.

Just days ago, doctors at Bagdad operated on CBS News reporter Kimberly Dozier, who had been wounded in a roadside bomb explosion on Memorial Day. They also treated ABC News correspondent Bob Woodruff, who suffered a head wound in January.

Like those featured in the recent HBO documentary Baghdad ER, doctors here say working at a battlefield hospital is at once the most fulfilling and most frustrating experience of their lives -one that has changed them, as doctors and as people.

The doctors say the dizzying rush of gravely wounded patients, famous or not, helps them hone their skills and build confidence. But ethical questions, such as the decision to keep Biggers alive, prompt them to reflect beyond the wounds to consider the wounded, their families and their loved ones.

"I hope this experience will remind me to dig into the personal lives of the patients I treat," urologist Jay Bishoff says. "They are not just men with gunshot wounds or kidney stones, but people with hopes, dreams and real fears."

Doctors say the reality here is different from anything back home: more brutal, more destructive, more angry. And, for at least four doctors, more personal.

Reality is the Marine begging orthopedic surgeon Paul "Chip" Gleason not to amputate his mutilated hand. "He reached up with his other arm and grabbed me and said, 'Don't take it,' " Gleason recalls.

Reality is the bloodied insurgent shot in the genitals by a U.S. soldier. Bishoff says he found little to repair, but he resisted urgings by angry GIs to amputate.

And reality is Biggers, the soldier with the bullet wound through his head, kept alive by doctors who wouldn't have operated on him back home. "It's not our job to play God," Schlifka explains. "Even if we know that functionally they will not recover, we feel that it is important for their families to have closure."

The pact between Bakken and Schlifka, though well-meaning, has left the Biggers family in an emotional limbo. Within hours of the surgery that kept him alive, Biggers was headed out of Iraq.

Today, he remains comatose at Walter Reed Army Medical Center in Washington, D.C. He reacts to noise and touch, and he opens his eyes occasionally, but they remain unfocused. Members of his family rejoice with every flicker of consciousness. They hope for a miracle.

"They've gone from saying 'let him die with dignity' to 'there is hope that the damage is not nearly as much' as they thought," says father Rand Biggers, 59. "They say these things are incremental."

Using a Montana law that allows for marriage by proxy consent, Rand Biggers arranged in April for his son to wed fiancée Britni Fuller, 20. The couple's son, Eben, was born Friday.

Rand Biggers wants to give Ethan every chance to live and believes the battlefield brain surgeons made the right choice to keep him alive.

"I would thank them with all my heart," he says, "even if this doesn't turn out well."

A searing request Gleason, the orthopedist, worried whether he could handle the combat hospital experience. "You talk to my wife, and she'd tell you that I was very nervous about coming over here, being able to do the job that's required," he says.

The 6-foot-4 surgeon - who carries his 9mm pistol into surgery because base procedures require even doctors to be armed at all times - leads one of the busiest teams in the hospital. Body armor protects a soldier's abdomen and chest, but bombs wreck arms, legs and faces.

Although Gleason overcame his jitters, he still struggles to get past the image of the young Marine pleading for his hand. Gleason says he knew that it could not be saved, and he had to make a choice about what to tell the Marine.

The surgeon told him he would save what he could. But in the end, that promise was empty, Gleason concedes. He amputated the hand.

"Nothing was savable beyond the wrist," he says. "That was probably the hardest time I've had. No one else has asked specifically those questions and made those requests. It's very difficult to face."

In retrospect, Gleason says, the promise and the momentary hope it gave the Marine were good.

Gleason and the other doctors look for ways to exorcise the images. They smoke cigars or watch The Princess Bride for the umpteenth time, reciting in unison many of the lines. Bishoff uses a punching bag to relieve stress. Maj. Raymond Cho, an ophthalmologist, plays classical music on his electric violin. Lt. Col. Eugene Ross, an ear, nose and throat surgeon from New York City, works out furiously.

"I run farther and faster than I ever have. I've taken a minute off my 2-mile run because there's so much nervous energy to burn off," Ross says. "Nothing prepares you for this. Nothing prepares you for the wounds of the 21st century."

A quandary unique to war

U.S. soldiers in Ramadi had watched for two weeks as an insurgent set about planting a roadside bomb. When he was finally placing the explosive in the ground, they shot him from a distance and wounded him in the groin, according to a report Bishoff read.

The wounded man managed to reach a car and flee. But he was captured five hours later, still bleeding from the wound, and flown to the hospital here.

Bishoff could have simply amputated the insurgent's genitals, which were mangled by a bullet from an Army sniper. At an Iraqi hospital, doctors would have had to remove the man's penis, Bishoff says. The U.S. soldiers who caught him planting the bomb had made clear that they preferred amputation, he says.

"My journal records that they said: 'Doc, why did you have to fix it? You could have thrown it all away,' " Bishoff says. "They didn't want me to reconstruct his penis. They didn't want me to reconstruct his testicles. They were hoping that I would just remove all of that."

Bishoff says he understood their anger. "The troops are actually seeing these insurgents in the field, men trying to kill them on a daily basis, and this grows a lot of hatred," he says.

Colleague Schlifka calls it a quandary only war could produce. As he puts it, "I don't usually care for my enemies in the U.S."

But the doctors say they have no choice. Their first duty is to the patient, even if the patient is the enemy. Even if front-line troops disagree, Bishoff says.

In surgery, Bishoff did what he considers some of the best work of his life. He says the man was belligerent after the operation and struggled with hospital technicians and nurses. Then Bishoff explained through a translator the hard work he had done to reconstruct the man's genitals.

"He completely calmed down," Bishoff says. "He says: 'Thank you very much. I know. I saw it. I looked down there. I saw that it was a terrible injury, and everything feels like it's normal and intact.'"

Col. Thomas Jefferson, medical ethics consultant to the Army surgeon general, acknowledges that treating insurgents can be a dilemma for doctors. But he cites a host of ethical directives - including the Hippocratic oath and requirements under the Geneva Conventions - that call for the best care regardless of who the patient is.

"Medicine transcends the politics of the day and all of the down and dirty things that are going on that cause the war in the first place," Bishoff says. "Above that, you have medicine, people who are sick, people who are injured and who cannot help themselves. And that's what we do."

Brain surgeons Schlifka and Bakken, with their shaved heads, look like bookends. Pasted around the hospital as a joke are photocopied pictures of Schlifka as "Dr. Evil" and Bakken as "Mini-Me" from the Austin Powers films.

Schlifka, a former powerlifter, wears a surgical cap adorned with a Grateful Dead pattern of skulls and roses. Married and the proud owner of two 200-pound mastiffs named Baloo and Thor, he enjoys lifting other doctors off the ground for birthday photos here.

Bakken, his 5-foot-6 alter ego, wears prescription ballistic goggles for his astigmatism. They make him look like a World War I fighter ace. Single and from Decorah, Iowa, Bakken stunned his family last year by giving up a civilian practice to volunteer for the Army. Then he extended a six-month tour to a year.

The doctors had a brush with fame after operating on Woodruff and cameraman Doug Vogt, who were wounded by a bomb Jan. 29.

Trauma and hope

Surgeons say that all patients receive the same care, whether American or Iraqi, civilian or military. But they admit that the Americans with dire wounds cause them the greatest distress. "It's like a guy from your hometown," Schlifka says. "These kids, they're behind the eight ball, tremendous amounts of bleeding, tremendous amounts of injury."

The doctors say they find hope in some of the head-injury cases.

"Hans and I have been surprised many times how these people have done and recovered," Schlifka says. "The mind-set that all these injuries are non-survivable is not true."

Biggers, the soldier from Beavercreek, Ohio, suffered excessive blood loss that led to a base-wide request for blood. The surgery lasted three hours. Schlifka and Bakken removed large sections of Biggers' skull to relieve swelling.

Today, his future remains uncertain. "When we first got here, the doctors really gave us absolutely no hope. They just said my brother was going to be a vegetable," says Liza Biggers, 24, who remains at her brother's bedside at Walter Reed. "(But) the nurses who have been there with patients and have seen the miracles say they've seen worse than Ethan walk out of here. I think he's fighting. I think he has everything to live for. So I think we ought to give him a chance."

The work of Schlifka and Bakken - their unique pact back at the battlefield hospital - gave the family the opportunity to hope.

"All I can do is the best I can do," Bakken explains. "I couldn't sleep at night if I didn't."

Tribute To A Fallen Soldier

# Chapter 71

———

# BOOTS OF WAR PROJECT FINISHED, PRINTED, HUNG

5/16/06

I started taking pictures of soldiers' boots and created a photo essay. This week, working with the Communications squadron, the essay was printed as a large poster and hung on the wall by the dining facility section of the hospital. A copy was sent to Colonel Taylor, several copies were sent home for me, and one was sent to the secretary of the Army. The poster generated some interest, and I was asked many questions like, Why boots? Why those boots? Why not my boots? I had been working on an explanation for the project and wrote the following to accompany the photo essay:

*Boots of War*
Photo Essay by Jay T Bishoff, Lt Col, USAF, MC
AEF 9/10 Baghdad Iraq 2006

I don't remember exactly where I saw the picture, but I do remember that I saw it just before deploying with the 332 EMDG in support of Operation Iraqi Freedom. I believe it was in a magazine showing the year 2005 in review. There were pictures of the hurricanes, tornados, tsunami disasters and then there was a humbling photo of a fallen soldier's boots, sitting on a simple wood platform, with dog-tags hanging motionless from an ammo clip. The soldier's M-16 was standing tall in the back, supporting a helmet that would no longer be needed. An American flag was on the stand folded neatly into a triangle. It was positioned on the right side of the M-16, with a Purple Heart medal on the left. No title was given, and no explanation needed. Before I could reel-in my imagination, my mind wandered to a home somewhere in the US, where a little boy would be looking through his house searching for not just any man, but looking for his father, a young soldier with strong, conditioned arms that used to lift him high in the sky when he came home from work. I moved away from those thoughts and for a few minutes looked at the details in the picture, but my thoughts wandered again to the realization that the fallen soldier's boots could be my boots, or the boots of anyone of us sent here in support of Operation Iraqi Freedom. All who are deployed are one sniper's bullet, IED, or mortar away from being that fallen soldier with boots on the battlefield cross's platform .

Within a week of seeing the picture of the fallen soldier's boots, I myself was in Iraq as the urologist for the 9/10 AEF rotation at the 332 EMDG hospital in Balad. On one of the first days there I met the vascular surgeon, a quiet, intelligent and humorous person who was wearing black wingtip dress shoes in the OR. I suggested that his real OR shoes were in the mail and that they would be a welcome change. He looked at me as though I should have known that all good surgeons wore dress shoes—wingtip dress shoes—in the OR, and for a second I was insecure about wearing my new Burkenstock rubber clogs that I had purchased specifically for this deployment and, I thought, much better suited for mucking around in blood, body fluids and the like in the OR than, say, dress shoes made for church and courts of law. I saw another surgeon who chose well-seasoned, even blood soaked running shoes, brought from home. Because of arrogance, he was not well liked by many of the other surgeons. He asked me to take a photo of his shoes "standing on a podium" and then jumped onto an air conditioning unit for the shot. A nurse had boots with the soles worn off, but secured with layers of duct tape.

Figure 38. Wingtip dress shoes worn by a vascular surgeon in the operating room.

Figure 39. Operating room nurse's boots before receiving her combat pay.

My encounter with interesting footwear (boots) was not limited to the operating room. In clinic, during my first week of deployment, I met a young Marine who had already been in the country for eleven months. He came by helicopter from a far away forward operating base to see me, for what turned out to be a minor problem with an easy cure.

During my examination I noticed that his boots were very worn and wanting to be helpful, I insisted upon writing a letter giving him permission to pick up a new pair of boots from supply while he was here in Balad.

"No thank you, sir!" he replied, "These are my lucky boots."

"Lucky boots?" I inquired. He explained that the boots on his feet, with the soles worn to the point of lacking any tread at all and sporting a single bullet track across the toe of his right foot, exposing the metal plate beneath the leather surface, were in fact his lucky boots. He went on to give a detailed description of different events during the eleven months of his deployment where he had survived nine IED attacks, all with significant vehicle damage, and seven small-arms fire fights. On one occasion when he had not been wearing those boots, on that unlucky day two of the members of his squad died in an IED blast. Since then he has worn his lucky boots everyday, and while he and his squad still experienced attacks and IED blasts, no one in his unit had perished, and the reason was clearly due to the magic of those boots.

"Sir," he went on to explain, "I have three other pairs of boots, but we are all better off if I just wear these."

Well, of course I agreed and stopped typing the letter to supply.

At that time, I was not in the habit of bothering people to shoot pictures of their boots, so I never did get a shot of the "lucky boots." But those boots and the fallen soldier's boots became the thrust behind this project. What I did do was start thinking about the boots in Iraq carrying so many different people, from so many different backgrounds, doing so many different jobs. There are many different professions required to fight this war and to support the men and women in harm's way. To use a tired saying, most of us are here to support those at the "tip of the spear." That is the tip of the spear thrust into the side of Iraq in an attempt to heal her from tyranny and protect us from terrorism. I would consider the medical support to be located along the shaft of the spear, somewhere toward the front, but certainly not the tip of the spear. So, the fighters and the supporters of the war became the focus of this essay.

There are seventy-nine pairs of boots surrounding one empty pair—those of the dead soldier. There is nothing symbolic about the number of photos. That is the number that seemed to fit the best. The images are somewhat randomly placed, sort of like Polaroid photos taken during the war that you might label for future reference and share with some friends who came over to your house to welcome you home from war. I had an image of a group of people sitting at the kitchen table telling war stories and showing the pictures, laying them out one at a time so all could see.

Each picture represents one of the different professions needed to support the warriors. Each photo has a white border symbolic of the physical, psychological and spiritual boundaries we all place between us and those around us, even those very close to us. The fallen soldier has no need for those boundaries, so there is no border around his picture, and the edges fade from color into the black background just as his or her life passed during the conflict.

Almost all of the different squadrons or organizations at Balad Air Base are represented on the poster. There is a heavy emphasis on the medical side of war, in part because this is my world and also because for the fallen soldiers, we are the last ones to deliver support and the last chance to prevent the image of the fallen soldier from becoming reality.

Despite all of the support offered in war there are fallen soldiers. In this case, despite the efforts of a lot of people, in fact seventy-nine different people, the soldier has indeed fallen, and in a sense, we are all affected by the failure of our best efforts to prevent the death of a comrade.

Among the supporting images is a photo of a nurse's old OR boots held together with duct tape and worn soles before she received her combat bonus. A second picture is of the same nurse, but with new shoes ordered a month after she started receiving combat pay.

Figure 40. Operating room nurse with new shoes she could afford after receiving her combat pay bonus.

These two pictures symbolize the changes and improvements that can occur in our lives during deployment. Many who participated in the war effort lost weight, saved money, got physically stronger, worked on relationships, smoothed out personality quirks or took pictures of boots, but the idea here is that of self improvement is an on going process not deterred by an environment of destruction.

The photo of the child's burned feet, titled "Needed Boots," are the feet of a beautiful Iraqi girl who stepped in the family cooking fire and was rushed to our hospital. When the anesthesiologist tried to administer general anesthesia, she tried to bite him in an effort to protect herself from something she feared.

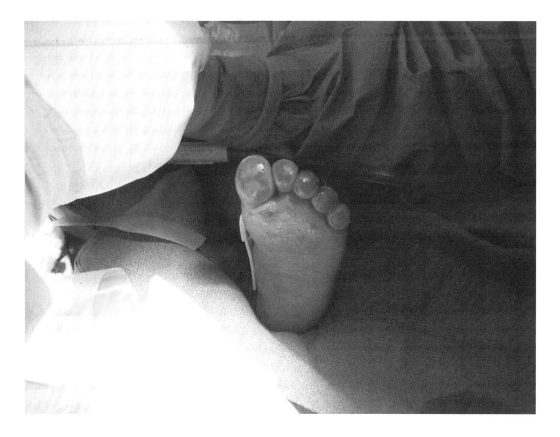

Figure 4I. Severe burns on the feet of a small Iraqi child who stepped into the family cooking fire.

A skilled plastic surgeon helped treat her, giving her the best care she could get any where in the world. The image of the painful burns on her toes is symbolic of the great price many children have paid during this conflict. Many schools throughout Iraq are closed, used and looted by insurgents, Iraqi military and police alike. Many Iraqi children suffer the pain of missing mothers or fathers who are dead. Many children have been injured by gunshot wounds and IED blasts, unable to be protected by a peaceful nation and solid government, similar to the little girl's feet that were unprotected by something as simple as boots, readily available back in our country, but not here.

Like any strong military organization the corners are supported by strong leadership, for us at the hospital and the base levels. Congress and civilian DOD leaders are represented, since they are also leaders responsible for our presence here. They are included to remind our political leaders what it means to commit troops to war.

There is symbolism represented by many of the images, but I won't ruin the chance for your own imagination to interpret them by telling you what each of them mean to me. Nevertheless, several should be brought to your attention. The fallen soldier's boots rest on two military wool blankets, taken off the shelf in the hospital. Most of the OR nurses insist on one blanket being on the bottom of the NATO cot, used to take fallen soldiers from the OR to the recovery unit or to the intensive care unit. The blanket on the top is symbolic of the concern for suffering, and the desire of the medical staff to offer warmth and comfort. The flag is folded in a triangle with a small amount of red showing. The flag is folded imperfectly and reflects the many small imperfections of war and the frequent loss of life sustaining blood seen in the hospital. Sandbags surround and support the platform as part of the protection offered many soldiers on the battlefield. The chain holds the dog-tags as a special reminder of home and faith recognized as significant only by the owner. Finally, the center stands between two tents one old and one new. We were told by the Secretary of Defense Donald H. Rumsfeld, "We go to war with the equipment we have." The new and old tents represent the fact that while we were trying to get new and better equipment, many soldiers suffered loss of limb and life.

So that should be far more than anyone ever wanted to know about why I would take a bunch of pictures of boots. The essay is not complete, and never will be completed. And that too is symbolic of this conflict and our involvement in Iraq. The poster is also incomplete because the aforementioned picture of the lucky boots is not included. Even though they will never be seen on the poster, every time I find a different pair of boots and think about the essay, I see the lucky boots worn by a short, tired, but very capable Marine and hope the lucky boots never stepped on to the fallen soldier's platform.

Figure 42. The first Boots of War poster was hung outside the hospital dining area. Many more would be printed and placed around Balad Air base.

"Boots of War" a photo essay by:
Jay T. Bishoff, LT COL, USAF, MC and Tung Trinh, AIC Graphic Artist.

C-17 Pilot

# Chapter 72

---

# FINALLY, HOPE FOR HOME

5/20/06

This afternoon I was thinking about what an incredible experience it has been serving our forces in Iraq with the remarkable group of selfless, dedicated staff that makes up the 332 EMDG during the AEF 9/10 rotation. I thought about all I had accomplished. Professionally, I performed 165 operations, most for kidney stones, but many for trauma to the ureter, bladder, testicles, and penis.

UROLOGICAL SURGERY CASE LOAD: ureteroscopy basket stone extraction, 45; ureteroscopy with laser lithotripsy, 18; percutaneous access to kidney, 5; exploratory laparotomy. 12; nephrectomy, 4; urethral injury, 7; bladder injury. 11; testis injury, 19; penis injury, 12; ureter injury, 2; and other cases, 29.

Before coming to the gulf, I had treated only minor genitourinary traumatic injuries but now have a wealth of experience with difficult, devastating injuries to the genitourinary system. Personally, I lost fifteen pounds while eating normal amounts but working out at the gym almost daily, lifting weights, running, and swimming. I have never felt better physically than I do now, and as I think about having lived about half of my life, it is a wake up call to take better care of what I have.

I finished the second edition of the *Bishoff Kavoussi Surgical Atlas*, which should be available in the fall of 2006. I finished a photo essay called "Boots of War." I served for four months as the group leader for the Church of Jesus Christ of Latter-day Saints servicemen's group. I finished reading the *Book of Mormon* from start to finish and most of the New Testament. I read, *Freakonomics*, *Shooter*, *Making of a Marine Corps Officer*, and *Honeymoon*. I kept journal entries compiling almost two hundred and fifty typewritten pages of stories and experiences.

At the 322nd we admitted 1,500 patients to our fifty-bed hospital, unloaded 608 helicopters, saw 2,500 patients in the ER, performed 2,500 surgical procedures, ordered 31,000 lab tests, used 3,422 units of blood (approximately 29 units a day), obtained 9,500 CT scans and plain films, filled 75,000 prescriptions, and served 72,272 meals—all in 120 days.

For the vast majority of us, nothing in medicine will be as rich and rewarding as our experience here. I was actually thinking I would miss the action and the entire experience.

When the staff from patient admission and dispositions gets a patient from the helo pad, they put him on a two-wheeled cot holder, feet first. They roll them off the landing pad along a sidewalk, and then walk past the open ER doors. They reverse their direction and wheel the patient into the ER head first, so they don't have to turn them once inside.

Figure 43. Air evacuation arrives with critically injured U.S. soldier being carried on a NATO litter as the attendants turn into the emergency department.

I was leaving the clinic and walking over to the ER and noticed a fresh red blood trail on the sidewalk outside the ER. Fresh blood is the expected red color. On the hot cement it quickly turns to a cedar redwood color, and then slowly fades until it is just a barely noticeable stain on the sidewalk. No one washes it away outside the hospital. It seems to take care of itself. This is a regular event that plays out about once or twice a week. Sometimes there is a lot of blood, a heavy line, and sometimes just a small trail with an occasional drop along the way.

Today it was a medium-sized trail leading from the helipad, past the OR door where the PAD rolls the stretcher to turn from feet first to head first as they enter the ER. Then the trail led back inside the double set of ER doors. Several techs from the ER were spraying disinfectant on the floor and mopping up a large pool of blood. In the ER, dressings are removed, wounds examined and scans or films ordered. The cots are made of a porous nylon that lets blood pass right through to the floor.

The trail of blood picked up again from the large pool on the ER cement floor but became much heavier leading down the hall because the patient had dressings removed. The trail followed the well-beaten path towards the CT scanner. Several hospital staff hurried along doing their jobs, skillfully avoiding the spill on the floor. Without even looking down they missed stepping into the blood and tracking it around the hospital. One of the few remaining radiology techs from our AEF 9/10 rotation recognized the inquiring look on my face.

"Nothing for you, Dr. Bishoff," he said. "Just another American with a gunshot wound to the head."

Just then it hit me. . . . I won't miss this at all!

Made in the USA
San Bernardino, CA
14 February 2013